Praise for
Compelling Conversations
with Dolphins & Whales
In the Wild

"I loved this entire book. It had me tearing up, laughing out loud, calling out "Oh My God!," and rejoicing again and again."
— Nina Shoroplova, Author, *Trust the Mystery*

"The author's work with dolphins in the wild might well be compared to Dian Fossey's work with gorillas in the wild. She also shows remarkable courage, wrapped in wit, wisdom, playfulness and knowledge."
— Jean Bjorgen [first edition]

"There is such a powerful and heartfelt presence to this brilliantly written book! It is all at once fascinating, thrilling, moving, humorous, stirring, tragic, enlightening, and hopeful! Many thanks to Bobbie Merrill for this revealing book in behalf of our wonderful marine life 'ohana' and planet. And, thanks, too, for offering all of us real hope!"
— Trish Campbell, Court Reporter, Author

"I am eternally grateful to Bobbie Merrill for sharing the dolphins' profound insights and stories in her delightful book, which is as fun to read as it is transformative."
— Cynthia Sue Larson, Physicist, MBA, DD,
Author, *Quantum Jumps* and *Reality Shifts*

"I didn't want this book to end."
— Susan Shoemaker, Owner,
Peninsula Web Design and Allé Face Oils

"This easy flowing and fascinating page-turner reminds me to deeply treasure all of the moments of my life and to protect our precious ocean that I both love and require for survival."
— Dr. Ron Pion, M.D., Medical Consultant

"A unique contribution to any Self-Help reading list. This blend of self-help healing and spiritual insight uses the therapist author's encounters with dolphins as a foundation for understanding how to learn to live with affection."
— Midwest Book Review [first edition]

"Glorious, and even the book healed me."
— Terrence Shaw [first edition]

"I believe your Kindness Movement could be an important movement—a truly important Movement!"
— Kathleen Gage, Marketing and Visibility Strategist

"This integrating model of *all* that is so urgently needed in our world *now* belongs in educational settings of all kinds and for all ages—including schools, libraries, universities, and on-line learning."
— Anne Adams, Ph.D., Corporate and Educational Consultant

"Lovely writing and a beautiful message."
— Lynne Klippel, Publisher, Author, *Women of Scar Clan*

Compelling

Conversations with

Dolphins and Whales in the Wild

Vital Lessons for Living in Joy and Healing our World

BOBBIE MERRILL

Parts of this book were first published by Beyond Words Publishing Co., Inc. in 1999, with rights sold to Germany, Japan, and South Korea; other parts were published in 2005 by Council Oak Books, LLC.

This third, broadly revised edition is published by GGM Publishing in 2020.

Cataloging-in-publication-data

Library of Congress Cataloging-in-Publication Data

Merrill, Bobbie Sandoz

Rev. ed. of: In the presence of high beings: What dolphins want you to know/Bobbie Sandoz.

p. cm. and

Rev. ed. of: Listening to wild dolphins. ©1999.

Includes bibliographical references.

ISBN: 978-0-5781928-5-7 (for the Paperback)
ISBN: 978-1-7344480-0-9 (for the eBook)

Non-Fiction

1. Adventure Memoir - Swimming with Wild Dolphins and Whales
2. Endangered Species - Animal Rights
3. Meditation - Healing
4. Quantum Physics - Manifesting
5. EFT - Anxiety and Trauma Treatment
6. Navy Sonar - Cetacean Strandings
7. Ocean Warming - Global Warming - Climate Change

Photos on Cover:
Shutterstock: Breaching Whale; Underwater Whale
Sarah Jones: Durban, South African Dolphins Surfing
Isaac Gautschi: Author Photo

~m~ A Gift from the Author ~m~

An Introduction to the
Dolphins' Manifesting Tips

Taken from the Author's EBook titled:

MANIFEST!

A Dolphin-Inspired Guide for Manifesting
Your Personal & World Dreams

BOBBIE MERRILL

A FREE PDF Download available at:
www.MakingRelationshipsWork.com

DEDICATION

With gratitude to the dolphins for their kind friendship, joyful wisdom, and loving patience with our slowness to listen to the language of other species and better worlds

Table of Contents

PART I

My Unexpected Discovery of Teachers Beneath the Horizon

PART II

Lessons from the Dolphins: Six Special Traits
of the Higher Self

PART III

Creating the World of Your Dreams: Six Insights for Manifesting Your Goals

PART IV

A Change of Subject: Giving Back to the Dolphins and Whales

PREFACE

I spent most of my adult years as a therapist, partnering with my clients in their efforts to unearth whatever obstacles they had inadvertently acquired to reaching their full potential and the depth of happiness they desired. Like me, most of them were essentially successful and happy people who simply wanted more. In fact, it was a mystery to me why there were so many of us who appeared to others to have found so many of life's answers, but in the privacy of our hearts, felt something was still missing.

And so, as I worked to help my clients uproot and remove their various barriers to achieving more joy, I pursued even deeper levels of happiness for myself. As a result of this quest in behalf of my clients and myself, I was able to uncover some powerful ways to fulfill the happiness we all sought. Yet, in spite of my success, there were still more pieces to the happiness puzzle that continued to elude me, much in the way they still eluded my clients.

When the story I'm about to tell first began three decades ago, in addition to not yet finding the last pieces to the happiness puzzle, I was faced with a new and more pressing problem in my life. My kids, who had brought so much aliveness and laughter to our home, were in the process of graduating from college and moving on in their own lives and out of our house.

To add to the challenge of adjusting to the loss of my children's regular presence in my life, my marriage was on shaky ground. In fact, my then-husband Tom Sandoz and I had gone so far as to separate and had announced our split to friends. Yet we continued to live as roommates in separate suites of a condo we couldn't sell and had somehow managed to rekindle our friendship enough to consider giving it one more go. But each time we thought our marriage might work, the friction between us would flare, and with each flare, our enthusiasm for continuing our off-and-on dance would fade again. Now, the vacuum created by our children's departure was shedding new light on the truth of our situation and the need to confront it.

Our condo was located in Honolulu, just a few miles from the Kahala Hotel—a favorite local spot where I loved to eat at their trendy snack bar, walk along the beach fronting the hotel, and visit their bottlenose dolphins that I had befriended at the beginning of Tom's and my separation.

Then, one day, following a larger-than-usual clash with Tom, I decided to drive to the hotel where I often went to soothe myself and visit their captive dolphins. Little did I know that a mystical event was about to happen at the hotel that day—one that would give me the courage I needed to face my next steps, while also unearthing my unspoken truth about the deeper, fuller life I yearned to live. Nor did I realize I was about to go on a significant journey that would give me the keys to the next level of happiness I had been seeking for my clients and myself—universal keys, as it turned out—that would work for anyone, no matter what state of contentment or fulfillment they had already reached.

This journey began with the hotel dolphins, followed by dolphins in the wild. Together, and in concert over the next ten years, they showed me six traits of the Higher Self that I later realized provide both the substance and the foundation for our human happiness. Along with these traits, the dolphins also showed me six unique insights able to help humans manifest their desires.

This special combination of traits and insights not only offer us a way to experience internal joy but also a way to fulfill our dreams. In short, they are the keys to our happiness that my clients and I had been seeking.

Of even greater value, while in the process of sharing these keys to our human happiness, the dolphins also revealed something that both surprised and inspired me: they revealed that the set of skills needed to live in true happiness and with success are the exact same skills needed to be our best selves and a greater humanity.

The simplicity of the dolphins' formula for achieving so much was initially a challenge for me to grasp. But, in time, I was able to see that even though their path to happiness and success is wrapped in the ease of fun, play, and joy—rather than the hard work I had been taught to expect—their simple keys are surprisingly able to propel humanity to much higher ground.

My clients and I (and others in our society) had been languishing for so long in our lesser selves that an opportunity to become much better people and a more evolved species was growing ever more important, if not urgent, for the sake of our imperiled salvation. In view of this urgency, removing the difficulty of becoming our best selves offered new hope, since an easier and more playful path might entice us to actually use it.

Understanding the full magnitude and urgency of this nudge from the dolphins for humanity to get going in the right direction before it's too late triggered a strong urge in me to share their simple keys to our happiness and greatness with my own species, hopefully in time to save the cetaceans and ocean as well as ourselves.

This motivated me to write a third edition of this book in order to share the dolphins' message once again—but this time with a clearer link to the ironic truth that pursuing deeper and kinder pathways to our personal joy and success offers us the unexpected keys to humanity's deliverance.

Compelling Conversations with Dolphins and Whales in the Wild: Vital Lessons for Living in Joy and Healing our World is the story of my unusual interactions with some of the wisest beings on our planet. It's also a story about the special traits of the Higher Self that dolphins and whales so clearly possess and how we can also adopt and use those traits—in conjunction with the insights they taught me—for manifesting the lives we most want to live. Finally, it's the story of how we can collectively use cetacean knowledge to take our species to the next level of our development and Higher Selves. This will not only result in our loving our lives more, but in bringing new light to our souls and the world.

I invite you to join me on this magical journey, during which the dolphins and whales will pull you into their hearts, as they did me, while teaching you the same life-changing lessons and keys to our happiness—and survival—that they offered me and asked that I share with you.

⁀

ACKNOWLEDGMENTS

I'm grateful to my second husband and soul mate, Dr. Tom Merrill—Tommy to me—who I consciously pulled to my life by using the dolphins' manifesting tools. I'm especially grateful to him for inspiring me to say yes to all of my dreams and to so fully and joyfully live our lives together.

I'm also grateful to my children, who not only inspired and nudged me to grow and be my best self from the moment they were born, but who developed into wonderful people who have enhanced my life and the lives of others and the world. They also helped me with their honest feedback and editing skills to improve this book—as did my wonderful sister, Dorothy Bremner, my special first-round editor and lifelong friend. I am also thankful to my baby sister Anne Gibson Galvan, for loving the dolphins and whales and their ocean home, and to other special friends, including Virginia Beckwith, Sue Thoele, Gail and Ron Pion, Mindy Finnegan, Lorna Jeyte, Kathy Muller Baldwin, Puchi Romig, Susie Wunderlich, Laurie Callies, Jo-Anne Lewis, Skip Wild Harrington, Patricia Casey Rogers, Virginia O'Neil, and many others who swam with me and/ or offered their insightful feedback, eager encouragement, and support, plus a few edits to both the book and my life. I'm further grateful to my particularly special grandchildren and their wonderful mother—as well as my stepchildren and step-grandchildren—for each of their varying roles in my life and for inspiring me to keep my eye on living the kind of life that will protect their futures and their joy.

I am additionally grateful to my readers for their interest in the dolphins and whales, for their caring about how we treat them and each other, for absorbing the cetaceans' startling lessons about reaching higher and becoming a greater humanity, and for joining me in doing all we can to help them and their ocean home survive.

Special thanks also go to our delightful web designers at Peninsula Web Designs, Susan and Ed Shoemaker, who not only inspire us, but who provide ongoing professional guidance and a truly beautiful and functional website. I am further grateful to Wendy Sorenson, Kathleen Gage, and Lynne Klippel for their early encouragement and help.

Thanks to Geoff Affleck, Publishing and Marketing Consultant (GeoffAffleck.com) for picking a great team and guiding our publishing experience with integrity and grace.

My deep gratitude and thanks go to the wonderful Jennifer Read Hawthorne (www.jenniferhawthorne.com), whose brilliance and professional editing magic pulled the message of *Compelling Conversations* into crisper focus and easier reading—even for me. I am further grateful to the gently wise and helpful Nina Shoroplova (ninashoroplova.ca) for her outstanding copyediting, proofreading, wisdom, and sharp eye in adding special touches of insight and clarity to *Compelling Conversations*. In fact, I consider the combined wisdom and gifts of Jennifer Read Hawthorne and Nina Shoroplova to be the final blessing drawn to this book.

I also greatly appreciate designer Angie Alaya's collaborative and artistic help with the cover. I am further grateful to the gently delightful and patient Amit Dey of Book Interior and Ebook Design (amitdey2528@gmail.com) for his expertise and caring help with the formatting.

Finally, I am grateful for God's presence throughout my experience of swimming with the enlightened dolphins and whales, and for bringing so much magic and grace to my life.

INTRODUCTION

What You'll Find in This Book

Compelling Conversations is divided into four parts.

Part I contains the full story of "My Unexpected Discovery of Teachers Beneath the Horizon." It starts with how I became acquainted with the dolphins—first at a hotel in Hawai'i and then in the wild—and the infusion of love in me that ensued. Part I also introduces my growing awareness of six special character traits that were consistently present in the dolphins I came to observe, know, and love.

In Part II, "Lessons from the Dolphins: Six Special Traits of the Higher Self," I share in greater detail the dolphins' special traits—all attributes that resonate with the Higher Self available to each of us. These include such qualities as kindness and friendship; playful humor and joy; harmony; exceptional intelligence used wisely; telepathic transparency; and the power of the heart.

Part III, "Creating the World of Your Dreams: Six Insights for Manifesting Your Goals," introduces six unusual insights about new ways to manifest our dreams that were unveiled during my extensive time with dolphins and whales. It also includes a chapter about four major trips I made to test the insights the cetaceans were giving me.

The final section of this book is Part IV, "A Change of Subject. Giving Back to the Dolphins and Whales." In it, I sound the alarm about what's at stake in our world—and why learning the lessons of how to become our best selves will not only make us feel happier and more fulfilled, but will also enable us to survive. I expose the source and harsh truth about the "mysterious" rise in the deaths of dolphins and whales—and talk about where their hope and ours lies.

I then share the scientific principle of "mirror neurons," what it would look like to engage them to start a wave of kindness—or even a full global Kindness Movement—and why the movement would work to stop cetacean deaths and so much more! Finally, I invite you to take an honest look at our destiny—both the cetaceans' and ours, for we are intertwined—and join the Kindness Movement as the last hope for all of our survival.

My hope is that the full scope of *Compelling Conversations*—from magic to holocaust—will not only dramatically enhance your personal life, but will awaken our species to the power and possibilities that living in our kindness and greatness offers. I hope that in the process, this book will show us how to survive. If enough of us band together as our best selves in the pursuit of a new world filled with caring, kindness, justice, and joy, we can create a tipping point that will carry all of us there.

A world filled with kindness is a *real* possibility that offers us *real* hope if enough of us get on board. So, read *Compelling Conversations* with this in mind, and see if you will be one of those who not only experiences new levels of personal power and joy as you read, but who will be drawn to contribute to a wave of kindness and a better world through either passive or active involvement.

Chapter quotes are mine unless otherwise indicated.

Spread love everywhere you go.

—Mother Teresa

PART I

My Unexpected Discovery of Teachers Beneath the Horizon

The planet desperately needs more peacemakers,
healers, and lovers of all kinds.
—His Holiness, The Dalai Lama

Although I first dove into the ocean simply to swim and play with the dolphins, I emerged ten years later with a precious collection of life-changing lessons that helped me to be a better person living a better life.

This book is designed to take you on the same journey I was blessed to enjoy so that you too can surface with some of the dolphins' magic in your own heart and life, while also helping to build a new world of kindness and magic for all.

New Teachers Introduce New Lessons

When I first began in 1989 to swim in the wild with dolphins and whales, life for me was good, but not nearly as good as it is now. Although I initially swam with my new friends simply for the fun of it, they surprised me with their remarkable level of intelligence, functioning, and altruism, which I had not realized cetaceans possessed and was initially reluctant to fully accept.

I was also suspicious of their ability to communicate with me and even more skeptical that their messages could improve my life. Moreover, the idea that dolphins could or would teach me—or anyone—an array of lessons is a challenging concept for most people to absorb, and I was no exception.

Thus, even when they gave me ample and repeated proof of their ability, first to converse with me and to then teach me complex concepts, my doubts about their capacity to do this lingered longer than was warranted.

But during the course of the next ten years and over two thousand hours of free swimming throughout the world with dolphins and whales, I was not only taken on a magical journey, but was also given a glimpse into the astounding world of wisdom in which the dolphins and whales dwell.

Although I persisted throughout most of this journey to seek repeated proof of the surreal abilities of the cetaceans, at last there was a turning point, and they won me over. That's also the moment when I made my final decision to write this book chronicling their lessons, which not only impacted my personal development, but also provided the missing pieces to the happiness puzzle my clients and I had been seeking. Even more surprising, they were also the pieces that had the ability to help my species become a greater, happier humanity, better able to survive.

Because of my own preliminary doubts about the dolphins' ability to teach me such valued lessons, I have included references to studies to support my observations. These will hopefully help readers to break through the same kinds of doubts I initially had so that they too can reap the full value of the lessons.

As a result of my eventual surrender to cetacean wisdom, I was able to accept and use the lessons they taught me about ways to dramatically improve my life. And it's those lessons I now share with you in *Compelling Conversations with Wild Dolphins and Whales* with the hope that you will benefit as much as I have.

"The dolphin's way is not to fall from grace
in the first place."

—Peter Russell

CHAPTER 1

The Dolphins Lure Me to Them

*Stay as aware of your thoughts and actions
as you would if a beloved master were
observing you, for this will prompt your Higher
Self to come forth in an effort to impress the
master, and in the process, draw life's
goodness to you.*

I needed to think. I needed to face the stark reality that my marriage was falling apart. So I headed for my favorite spot at the Kahala Hotel, where I often went to do my thinking and to soothe myself. Normally, I went to this special spot alone, but on this day, Tom wanted to go with me to walk along the beach together with the hope we might have a successful conversation to clear up the mess of the fight we had just had. But, it didn't take long before we engaged in yet another one of our spats that had been recently escalating, so Tom elected to wait in the restaurant until I was ready to leave.

The Lagoon Dolphins Open a New Door

Rather than finish my walk, I decided to visit the hotel's dolphins that I had befriended at the start of our separation. So, I found my favorite cluster of smooth rocks at the edge of the dolphins' lagoon fronting the interior units and gardens of the hotel and nestled myself into them. As I watched the dolphins glide through the water, rather than feel soothed as I usually did, I felt increasingly unsettled by my growing awareness that my marriage was about to collapse. Facing the truth of this led to rising worries over how I would cope and what to do next. I had committed the greater part of my adult years to this union, and the thought of calling it quits and finishing life's journey on my own stirred up new layers of disquiet in me.

As I anxiously imagined living alone in a less secure and pleasant condo, one of my favorite dolphins, Maka, swam toward me with a tourist's visor tucked under his fin. He then barely released the visor before quickly diving under the water to retrieve it and then drop it again. As I puzzled over what Maka was doing, he surfaced directly in front of me with the hat askew on his head and his eyes dancing impishly into mine. Taken aback by his silly image, I began to laugh. Maka seemed quite pleased with this result and repeated his trick over and over until I was able to forget about my fears of the future and surrender to simply enjoying his show. I wasn't sure at the time why the hotel dolphins had such a soothing effect on me, but I knew that our growing bond over the past few years had relieved some of the loneliness of my fading relationship. Once Maka had accomplished his mission, I stood to leave. But as I was gathering my things, I noticed that the dearest of my dolphin friends, Iwa, was slowly approaching me from the other end of the lagoon, so I waited to greet her. The moment Iwa got to where I was standing, she uncharacteristically positioned herself upright in the water before me and held this position for a full minute or so, while locking her gaze directly into mine. I had never seen Iwa sit upright before, nor had she ever looked at me in this direct, frontal manner. Her more typical side gazes were always very penetrating, but now she seemed to be looking both at and past me, to something beyond, as if reading the entire energy field surrounding my body and head.

As I pondered Iwa's unusual behavior and what she might be seeing, she sent a strong surge of love from her heart to mine. I felt mysteriously honored by this outpouring of love coming from Iwa and the upright position she continued to hold as she kept her gaze fixed on me. Although I was perplexed by its meaning, whatever it was, the mixture of Iwa's deep soulful gaze and the strength of her kind energy prompted a stream of tears to well up in me. When these long-held tears finally broke through to spill their warmth down my cheeks, the intensity of my fear of living on my own seemed to wash away with them.

I had not started to visit the hotel dolphins until a few weeks after my separation from Tom, and it was during my first visit that a special friendship with Iwa began when she dashed over to greet me upon my arrival. She repeated this behavior every time I visited and would then glide back and forth in front of me with an unblinking eye fixed on mine as I gazed with equal intensity back at her. I often felt locked into these gazes and lost in a dreamy trance as Iwa would continue to pull me through the portals of her eyes into the gentleness of her heart.

I realized that these gazes were rapidly drawing me out of my awake, beta state and into the more relaxed alpha realm I experienced while meditating. Next, they would pull me even deeper through the ranges of alpha into a slower theta trance, just short of slipping all the way into the dreaminess of a delta sleep state. These experiences matched the special times I had successfully fallen into deep meditation, and I was in awe of how quickly Iwa was able to pull me into the same dopamine-drenched state that had taken me years to achieve while sitting on my couch.

Next, Iwa would aim the top of her head toward me in a deliberate manner, as if to scan my body or send me some of her healing energy before turning back to look at me again. We would then resume our gaze and remain locked and lost in the moment, as she pulled me even more deeply into the cadence and symphony of her brainwaves and heart.

In time, I learned to send her love from my heart as well, and I always came away feeling as though I were emerging from the fullness of a soothing meditation. Although I had noticed that Iwa seemed to be the most conscious dolphin in the lagoon, it wasn't until years later that I learned she had been born and raised in the wild before her capture. During those extra years in the ocean with her family, Iwa had been given a unique opportunity to learn things from them that dolphins born in captivity or captured while still very young do not have the chance to learn.

I felt a good deal lighter and more at peace after spending some playful time with Maka, followed by my deeper than usual connection with Iwa. When I then walked with renewed serenity to the restaurant where Tom was enjoying a soda and the view, we were both happy to let go of our disagreement and move on.

Dolphins in the Wild

Soon after that healing evening with the lagoon dolphins, I met a man who had been free swimming with a group of wild dolphins in the waters off of Diamond Head. They had been meeting with him just a short distance down the beach from the hotel and to the left of the famed Diamond Head Point separating Waikiki Beach from the Diamond Head lighthouse and a strip of luxury real estate. He reported that although dolphins are not mentioned in the early lore of Hawaiians, several groups of them were now beginning to appear to boaters, and some were even meeting with swimmers off the shores of our beaches and bays.

I later learned that the reason we hadn't heard about people connecting with Hawai'i's dolphins prior to this is because close and personal encounters with cetaceans was a new phenomenon that was only recently taking place in Hawai'i and throughout the world. Although evidence shows that dolphins interfaced with the Greeks during the Renaissance and that individual dolphins have sporadically met with humans during subsequent centuries, pods of dolphins meeting with humans on a regular basis didn't begin until the mid-1980s.

Upon learning about these more frequent meetings, it dawned on me that dolphins had been swimming in the ocean with us during our days of body and board surfing as kids. But during that period of growing up in Hawai'i, my friends and I weren't aware that dolphins lived in our waters, so we failed to notice them on the days they were nearby or periodically surfacing to peek at us. And, on the rare occasion when we saw their fins bobbing up and down along the horizon, we simply assumed they were sharks and quickly exited the water. We didn't realize at the time that the up-and-down motion of the fins we saw moving through the water were actually quite different from the side-to-side motion used by Hawaiian sharks or the straight-line movement of the great white shark (rarely seen in Hawaiian waters).

Excited by the idea of participating in this new adventure of swimming with dolphins, I invited a group of friends I had grown up with in Hawai'i to join me in a search for our Hawaiian spinners, known for their ability to spin their bodies joyfully into the air. My friends were also eager to connect with the dolphins we had failed to notice as kids, and though we had great fun during our trips to various islands in pursuit of them, we didn't encounter any dolphins during those first efforts—other than once hearing their chirps, letting us know they were nearby, (which I later learned was their way of teasing us). Although we didn't know it at the time, each of us would ultimately have a number of very special encounters with dolphins and whales, most of them separately, but one of them as a group celebrating one of our birthdays.

Mine began when I heard about a handful of people who were swimming with a second pod of O'ahu spinners on the opposite side of the island from the Diamond Head group. Ironically, their beach was located in the rural area where I was born and had lived for a year—so I was even more drawn to swim with this particular pod.

Because Tom's interest in the dolphins was also piquing, we decided to go to their beach together in hopes of an encounter.

Unfortunately, as Tom and I began our drive to Makua Beach the next day, we engaged in another one of our spats and then drove in moody silence for the remainder of the trip. Although the dolphins were reported by others to have been playing with swimmers in the water prior to our arrival, they had left the area just before we got there. When this pattern repeated the following week, we began to suspect that our irritable energies might be repelling these good-natured beings. Our hunch was confirmed by a swimmer familiar with the dolphins, who reported that they approach some people right away, but make others wait before connecting. This pattern seemed to offer those being rebuffed an opportunity to become more conscious of what quality in them might be unattractive to the dolphins, a quality they would benefit from correcting.

As I began to reflect on what in me might need improving, it didn't take long to uncover the problem. Tom's and my energies had become unpleasant as we each looked to the other to change if we were going to save our marriage, rather than address what in ourselves might need correcting. When I shared this possibility with Tom, he agreed. So we committed to driving to the beach later that day without bickering about our rising irritations with each other.

Once we arrived, we didn't see any dolphins as hoped, so we paddled our kayak out into the water, where we sat calmly talking in more depth than usual. By each taking responsibility for our part in the problems between us, rather than continuing to blame the other, our communication was kinder and clearer than it had been for some time. When we returned to shore, others reported that the dolphins had been circling in a wide swath around us the entire time we were sitting in the kayak, and although we hadn't seen them, it was clear that their presence had impacted our communication.

Following this experience, we both knew that whether or not we stayed together, we would treat each other with more care. This was the beginning of my experience with wild dolphins, though I had not yet swum with them. And even though they had exerted a profound impact on me as I sat in a kayak in their midst that day, these brilliant and beautiful beings were just getting started. Tom and I decided to return to the beach the following day in hopes of making an even closer connection with these friendly and profound Makua Beach dolphins.

*Whenever you're filled with attractive energies,
the goodness of life will feel pulled in your
direction and, in time, will draw near enough to
share its blessings with you.*

CHAPTER 2

Profound Teachers

An assemblage of dancing dolphins are coming to the world's shores to inspire humanity by sharing their secrets for finding happiness and joy.

ollowing a peaceful drive to the beach the morning after Tom and I had successfully remained calm with each other while sitting in our kayak, we found a good parking space at the edge of the water. As we were parking, a single dolphin leapt playfully out of the water just a few feet from shore, and at the top of his leap, he glanced briefly in our direction. We had never seen a dolphin come that close to the beach, and we quickly sensed that he had come to herald our first swim with the dolphins that day.

Unexpected Lessons

My breath quickened as I sensed this call to play, and we both excitedly collected our snorkels and fins. But by the time we got organized and made our way to the beach, a handful of swimmers were emerging from the water, all talking at once about their vigorous swim with the dolphins and feeling ready for a rest.

My heart sank with worry that we had come too late, but I tried to keep my thoughts upbeat as we grabbed our gear and ran to the water's edge. By now, my heart was racing, and my breath was short and shallow. Although I realized I was on the verge of hyperventilating, I entered the water without any of my usual indecision or concern about the cold.

The moment I submerged my head in the water, I could hear a dolphin chirping. I chirped back through my snorkel, and he answered in turn. I responded again, and we chirped back and forth to each other until I began to giggle. His voice clarified where the dolphins were, and I swam cautiously toward the sound, being careful not to disturb them in the event I got near enough for an encounter. Yet whenever I got close to the origin of the chirping, the sound seemed to shift and come from another direction. At times, I lost contact altogether, and I began to feel as though I were being teased. No sooner would I give up on seeing the dolphins and head for shore than they would make their presence known by resuming a loud chorus of chatter.

Although I'm a strong swimmer, I eventually grew tired. Realizing that the dolphins were deliberately hiding, I was reminded of others' reporting that dolphins enjoy toying with people by playing hide-and-seek. When I first heard that claim, I assumed people were projecting more onto the dolphins' ability to organize a game than was plausible. But now, I laughed aloud into my snorkel as it dawned on me that I was, in fact, being intentionally teased.

Tom was also in search of the dolphins, and in his usual independent fashion, he had swum out toward the horizon as far as he dared. From time to time, he would stop to scan the ocean, looking in all directions for the elusive dolphins. But he too was being avoided.

Eventually we were able to concede that neither of us had succeeded in attracting the dolphins, so we bobbed in the water discussing whether or not to go back to shore. As we meandered slowly in the direction of the beach, we looked more carefully at the fish below, taking time to point out various sea creatures to one another. In the process, we discovered that although the fish and their surroundings were wonderfully enchanting, we had been completely overlooking them in our search for the dolphins. Now, as we started to relax and focus on the full magic of the ocean, we were better able to appreciate what we had right in front of us, rather than chase after what wasn't there.

Once relaxed, I began to notice that anytime I felt my heart flood with affection for the fish in the area, they would stop swimming in the direction they were headed and turn around to swim toward me. Whenever my heart opened even further or I began to coo at them through my snorkel, they would cock their little heads to peer at me and then swim even closer. I was so absorbed in my pleasure with this discovery that I forgot about my failure to attract the dolphins. Tom noticed what I was doing and also began to relate to the fish.

After releasing our feelings of fear and disappointment that the dolphins hadn't shown up, coupled with our new appreciation for the beauty of the reef and fish in our presence, we were unexpectedly rewarded by two dolphins silently appearing out of nowhere to park themselves immediately below us. Then two more swam alongside us. Then three more. I felt simultaneously euphoric and unsettled by the impact of seven large dolphins right next to me. But, the dolphins' calm and loving energy quickly quelled my fears.

They glided slowly by us in pairs and threes, establishing eye contact before gazing unwaveringly into our eyes, as if in a trance. It was clear that we were being rewarded for our commitment to holding onto our pleasant and positive energy. Not only did they offer peaceful friendship, as I had hoped, but their slow gliding speed and languid gazes all served as pacifiers that helped to calm my concerns. As I gazed into the eye of the dolphin who came closest to me, it seemed as though some extraordinary being lived behind his gaze and had come to say hello and welcome me to his world. I was enveloped by his kindness and could feel my body flood with the elation of pleasure hormones.

Before long, my heart was spilling over with love, and the urge to chuckle bubbled up from my soul. I heard myself cooing and chirping at times, followed by a whooping "Yee-ha!" at others. A level of glee I had not yet experienced engulfed me, as I realized I was being showered by the grace of God moving through the dolphins to surround and embrace me.

I had heard others describe wild dolphin encounters as comparable to swimming in champagne distilled from joy, and I now understood their search for an apt metaphor to describe such euphoria. As I surrendered to the pleasure, pure joy shimmered up from my soul in the form of rich, giggly laughter. Then the dolphins slipped away as suddenly as they had arrived. Tom and I surfaced to remove our masks and laughingly agreed that we were at last sated. We headed for the shore.

The Teaching Begins

As I drifted off to sleep that night, it dawned on me that the dolphins had started the process of teaching me lessons during my first encounter with them. These early lessons about using the power of contentment, harmony, and play to attract the things we most desire were especially meaningful to me because of my search for the keys to more fulfillment and happiness for my clients and myself.

But it wasn't until further into my decade of swimming with the dolphins (and later with the whales) that I realized they were also devising ways to show me how I could embody the same character traits of the Higher Self they possess as the easiest, most joyful and effective way for me to be attractive to my dreams of a good life. I was even more surprised when I later realized they were also teaching me how I could merge these Higher Self traits of attractiveness with a few simple tools to increase my ability to also manifest my specific desires.

Over time, I could see how much the dolphins' lessons were not just showing me the source of their own renowned magic, but were also teaching me how to bring more magic to my own life. In time I could also see that their lessons offered a surprisingly simple formula that humanity could use to create a society filled with the qualities of wisdom, love, harmony, and joy in our land-based world, parallel to what the dolphins have created just a few feet beneath the horizon's thin veil that divides our world from theirs.

Partway into my experience with the dolphins, I sensed that I was being urged to share these traits and insights with others and felt compelled to write about them. In fact, this urge was often so strong that I would dangerously write down a flood of ideas pouring through me as I drove home from the beach following a swim with the dolphins.

In the midst of this process, it occurred to me that these dancing dolphins were coming to our world's shores not only to inspire humanity to reach higher and do better, but to also share their secrets for how we can become our best selves in concert with finding the happiness we seek.

Once the seeds of tomorrow's desires are planted, enjoy the harvest of today's dreams—for gratitude and joy in present moments become magnets that attract God's grace to you, and tomorrow's dreams draw closer while you play.

PART II

Lessons from the Dolphins: Six Special Traits of the Higher Self

Giving is the highest expression of potency.

—Erich Fromm

Following my first connection with wild dolphins, I was hooked on spending more time with them. And to my delight, indulging in this pastime over the next ten years revealed more and more about how they had cultivated the magnetism that drew me to them in the first place. Not only did the dolphins have a strong, charismatic pull on me, and on others, but once we were drawn into their presence, they seemed to enjoy teaching us how they generate their powerfully positive force field and how we can learn to do the same.

The Source of Dolphin Magnetism

From the beginning of my time with the dolphins, I was not only clobbered by the power of their magnetic presence, but while in that presence, I was able to see that their legendary charisma comes from the purity of their hearts. Over time, I noticed that this purity is a result of their consistent expression of six special traits—each representing a facet of the Higher Self. And, it's this collection of Higher Self traits woven into the tapestry of a dolphin's character that appears to be at the core of their renowned magnetism.

Whenever a group of dolphins—each filled with these traits of the Higher Self—come together, they're collectively equipped to generate a powerful force field of loving energy traveling through the water, into which anyone crossing their path is irresistibly drawn. Whenever several pods merge, this force field is multiplied and becomes even stronger; and, on the special occasions when dolphin or whale pods—or a combination of both—come together to form superpods of up to a thousand cetaceans or more, the power of the positive energy they generate becomes an inordinately potent force.

In the next six chapters, I will reveal not only how the dolphins embody these six special traits of the Higher Self, but how they share these traits with us and entice us to use them. I will also show how these qualities not only serve as the source of the dolphins' and whales' loving and alluring natures, but lie at the heart of their legendary "magic"—a magic that we too could enjoy, simply by adopting these traits. So as you read this section, try on the idea of embodying the traits of the Higher Self for yourself and imagine the impact they could have on your life.

When you contact the Higher Self, the source of power within, you tap into a reservoir of infinite power.

—Deepak Chopra

CHAPTER 3

Trait #1: Unfailing Friendship and Kindness

*To the dolphin alone, beyond all other, nature
has granted what the best philosophers seek:
friendship for no advantage.*

—Plutarch

The first quality of the Higher Self I noticed in the
dolphins was how consistently they offer loving
kindness and friendship to humankind. As I personally received this gift of comaraderie from them, I was
struck by how enthusiastically and openly they offered it
to me and offer it to others.

The Endurance of Dolphin Friendship and Kindness

The gesture of cetacean kindness and friendship dates back to
ancient times, as revealed in the legends and art of Minoan,

Greek, and Roman cultures. Although we've tended to view these early reports of cetacean contact with humans as mythical, current reports of dolphin kindness lift these records from the realm of fantasy and restore them to their rightful place in a reality we can now observe and experience for ourselves.

Social psychologist, Dr. Jean Houston, astutely notes that the advent of dolphins' coming to our shores seems to coincide with times when humanity is in need of enlightenment and prior to periods of renaissance. Her theory is interesting in view of modern dolphins first showing up around the time our society was escalating our programs for spewing sonar into the ocean, while also becoming entangled in senseless wars across the globe. It was clearly a time when we were in dire need of the dolphins' lessons for teaching us how to be our best selves.

Pioneers of Dolphin Friendship

Although dolphin friendship with humans reaches far back in time, the current trend toward increased contact did not begin until four decades ago. The dry spell was broken in 1974, when an individual dolphin befriended Dr. Horace Dobbs in waters off the British Isles. Dr. Dobbs named his new friend Donald and was so affected by their interactions that he left his medical practice to write about their interspecies friendship and to dedicate his life to conducting affirming studies on the healing capacities of dolphins, particularly on their ability to lift people out of intractable depression.

When I met the congenial Dr. Dobbs twenty-three years later at the Sixth International Cetacean Conference in Australia, I understood why Donald had chosen him. When I later sent him the first edition of this book (*In the Presence of High Beings*), Dr. Dobbs shared that his studies confirmed our compatible beliefs in the high intelligence, telepathic skills, and healing abilities of dolphins.

Following Donald's friendship with Dr. Dobbs, Jojo, the best known of the individual, sociable wild dolphins, appeared off the coast of the Turks and Caicos Islands to befriend Dean Bernal, a San Diego marine aficionado and environmentalist. Like Dr. Dobbs, Dean was so enthralled by his connection with Jojo that he moved from California to the islands in order to continue their close friendship, which later included a Golden Labrador named Toffee, followed by many other dogs and people as shown on Jojo Internet sites.

An Acceleration of Dolphin Friendship

Following these initial encounters in the mid-1970s with these two solo dolphins, contacts with other individual and small groups of dolphins rose gradually over the next twenty years into the mid-1990s. Encounters then exploded and rapidly increased, and by 2000 there were numerous pods meeting regularly with people all over the world.

I had my first dolphin encounter with the Hawaiian spinners in 1989, fifteen years after Donald approached Dr. Dobbs and ten years prior to the exploding wave of contacts. Due to my timing, I was blessed to be involved before commercialism and large crowds altered the purity of the experience and was thus privileged to observe completely wild dolphins prior to their exposure to so much human contact.

When I first swam with the dolphins during this uncharted period of interspecies friendship, I was amazed by the variety of ways they found to share their kindness and friendship with me and others through humor, teasing, teaching, and play. Here's just a sampling of what I witnessed.

How Dolphins Initiate Friendship

Today's modern dolphins and their larger whale cousins come to our world's harbors, beaches, and bays, beguiling, calling, jumping, and teasing until people join them for a wealth of interactions, learning, healing, and play. They also bound toward our boaters, kayakers, paddle-boarders, and surfers in the open ocean with a glee and exuberance that portends their desire for friendship.

I have personally experienced these welcoming encounters with dolphins, ranging from large superpods swimming alongside and beneath our boats to individuals or small groups connecting with us in the water. I have also enjoyed more intimate interactions with both dolphins and whales, including close, personal contact and all manner of games, teasing, and high-level lessons.

Dolphins clearly let us know of their interest in our camaraderie by the way they bound toward us—jumping, spinning, wiggling, tail-slapping, and fin-waving, all while glancing playfully at us in their uniquely "flirtatious" way. Once they arrive, they will often continue to leap and spin and dance around us, sometimes even jumping over a small boat or a swimmer as they chirp and chatter with delight or engage us in brief eye contact or long, penetrating gazes. They may even raise their bodies out of the water unexpectedly right next to us in a burst of joy. Or they might wow us with a backflip or somersault or a surprisingly high leap up to twenty feet in the air. The greatest feat of all was a humpback whale rising out of the water in front of my car parked at the Diamond Head Lookout to do a backward tail walk. Although we see dolphins do this in marine park shows, I've never seen a wild dolphin do it and was shocked by the sight of a forty-ton whale accomplishing this right before my eyes.

Following these initial friendly and dramatic connections, dolphins will usually remain with us anywhere from five minutes to three hours or more. During this time, they may continue their acrobatics and vocalizations. Or they might swim slowly and in synchronization alongside us in the water, present their babies to us, or show us how to dive or spiral with them. Some bring fronds or debris to swish in front of us or to pass back and forth among themselves or with us. Most strive to communicate in a variety of ways or play various games designed to tease, play, and provoke us to laugh. Others imitate our sounds, smiles, and laughter or respond to our vocalizations and songs, which they like to echo back and forth with us, while sometimes following and sometimes taking the lead.

Whenever a dolphin decides to connect with you at a deeper level, he will engage you in more prolonged eye contact. Once this eye-to-eye alliance is established, he then locks you into his unblinking gaze and holds you there with him, heart-to-heart, for as long as three to five minutes or more. During these encounters, it feels as though a pathway without barriers between the two of you has opened, as the dolphin claims your heart for the time you are engaged. His gaze is similar to the tender look of other wise beings as they look into your soul and both see and love you as you are.

After engaging with a dolphin in one of these gazes, I am able to energetically recognize that particular dolphin whenever I see him or her again, even if I have no idea what that dolphin's physical characteristics are. It's as though we have gazed beyond the surface into each other's essence and are now friends, essence to essence. Wise teachers have suggested that we can heal the world by looking at each other in this deeply open and loving way.

Paying Friendship Forward

In addition to dolphin friendliness triggering a flood of positive hormones in us—including oxytocin, serotonin, dopamine, and endorphins—(as found in the bloodwork of people who've swum with them), studies show that these friendly encounters evoke an accelerated desire in humans to act with more benevolence and goodwill. As a result, the greatest benefit of being exposed to the degree of love and kindness the cetaceans offer is that it triggers within us an inclination to also want to be loving and kind.

Just imagine what our human society would be like if we adopted this Higher Self trait of kind friendship and love at the level the dolphins offer us, triggering in others the desire to also adopt it. Take a moment to really imagine what our species and world would be like if enough of us assumed this Higher Self quality of unfailing kindness and friendship, and then see if you would like to adopt this quality and be part of a promising and powerful trend.

Let loving kindness and friendship flow from your heart toward all things in the same way the sun shines everywhere without discernment. Not only is this ability in dolphins the source of their magic, but the friendship they offer makes life on this planet considerably more joyful.

CHAPTER 4

Trait #2: Playful Humor and Joy

Humor and play form the foundation of joy.

The second gift of character I regularly witnessed the dolphins embody is the gift of playful humor and joy. And, due to this delightful trait that permeates their entire natures, dolphins bring extra doses of fun with them wherever they go. Initially, I simply took pleasure in the dolphins' generous outpouring of this enchanting quality. But over time, I fell in awe of their ability to maintain a state of euphoria on such a continuous basis and at a level so far above what humanity has achieved. I was also struck by the positive impact this level of joy has on the world around them and on those blessed to be in their presence.

The Joy of Fun

When I first began to analyze how dolphins are able to maintain so much bliss, I noticed that their joy is based primarily on their enthusiasm for humor and play and a tireless commitment to fun. Following are some of the ways the dolphins pursue fun during their time with us, which not only adds to their joy and ours, but also triggers the release of our pleasure hormones at levels that enhance both our physical and emotional health.

Joyful Welcoming

Dolphins would often initiate invitations for us to play with them with such exuberance and joy that we invariably felt engaged in play before we even got started. For example, on the days when they wanted to play, they might acknowledge our arrival by leaping into the air the moment our car could be seen from the beach. Or, they might make a full U-turn off the course they had been traveling to bound enthusiastically shoreward toward us, as if greeting old friends. This kind of unguarded and full throttled welcome is one of the many ways dolphins exude a sense of enthusiastic playfulness and contagious joy.

Performing to Evoke Joy

After so warmly welcoming us, the dolphins would then initiate a variety of playful activities, most commonly filled with the element of shock. For instance, they might hide in silence long enough for us to conclude that they weren't going to show up, then terrify us into hysteria with an unexpected leap out of the water right next to us, followed by repeated jumps all around us filled with extra wiggles and spins and a cacophony of squeals.

Or, they might move us to joy with their performances by achieving more than we thought they could manage.

I witnessed a particularly entertaining one of these appearances taken to the limit in the Dominican Republic when a young whale calf approached our small boat full of onlookers and began to jump repeatedly to our applause. With each jump, he managed to hang an extra moment in the air while holding prolonged eye contact with us to make sure not to miss a moment of our pleasure in his triumph. Then, just when we thought he couldn't possibly continue, he would make yet another jump, each one fully clearing the water as his pectorals flopped adorably to the side. This calf was noticeably stagestruck, and after managing to complete fifteen full jumps, it was clear that he was hooked on bringing joy to humans.

Another playful performance involved five baby dolphins off the Big Island of Hawai'i who also enjoyed bringing pleasure to their human audience. They were riding without their mothers in the bow waves of our boat, which had slowed down enough while we were deciding what to do next to enable them to safely hop into our bow wave to ride. These babies seemed quite pleased with their solos and became extra wiggly whenever our crowd marveled at their independence and skills.

One was adept enough to dare to jump while in the midst of surfing our bow wave, which drew great cheers from our crowd. Seemingly smitten by our applause, he proceeded to jump again and again and then higher and higher, as we hooted and hollered "*hana hou!*" (Hawaiian for "bravo, one more time, do it again!"). This adorable young dolphin clearly took pleasure in the delight and laughter of his happy audience, and to our amazement, he kept jumping. One of his buddies got hooked on the idea and joined in.

Then another tried it as well. But only the first jumper was able to coordinate his jumps with glances at us, and toward the end, he included some prolonged, flirty looks and a little kick to his jumps, adding to our laughter and joy.

Eventually our captain began to increase our boat's speed slightly, causing the babies to drop out one by one. The talented jumper was the last to leave, and as he did, he surprised us all by leaping a full ten feet into the air, while sneaking a self-satisfied peek at us from the top of his jump. When this elicited another eruption of hollers, he did it again, then again and again, as he danced his way out of our bow wave, raising the level of our cheers a few decibels. This dolphin seemed to take extra pleasure in provoking our joy as his skills developed before our eyes. He was clearly on his way to stardom on the playful stage of shared interspecies joy.

After this baby had completed his performance, an adolescent leaped twenty feet out of the water to bring down the house. The adolescent then continued to make twenty-foot jumps repeatedly, as we screamed "*hana hou*!!!" louder and louder with each jump. We were sure he couldn't do another, so we were as surprised as we were delighted each time he popped out of the water to leap again. This lasted for about twenty more jumps as the pod moved away from our boat toward the horizon.

The Play of Bow Riding

In addition to the baby dolphins bringing us so much pleasure while riding our bow wave, adult dolphins are the most frequent riders of the waves and wakes formed by our boats. During bow riding, there's always a special exchange between the dolphins and boaters, as we offer them the gift of our waves to ride and they respond by sharing the joy of their play with us.

Often, a dolphin will flirt with a person on board while bow riding, and I'm always delighted when they catch my eye. One of the more special of these connections came during a time when I was engaged in my ongoing debate with myself as to whether dolphins are truly telepathic. I was still riding the fence on this topic at a time when a friend and I were enjoying a group of Hawaiian spinners playing in the bow wave of our boat. My friend noticed that one of the dolphins had a V cut out of the center of his dorsal fin and promptly named him Notch. When she asked him aloud if there were other dolphins sporting notches, Notch quickly left his spot at the front of our bow by diving deeply into the water and out of sight. After searching for him for a minute or so, I looked at her as if to say, I guess not.

We then began to worry that he had left due to feeling embarrassed or hurt by her question, but a few minutes later, Notch returned with a friend, also sporting a notch on his dorsal. My friend and I squealed with a mixture of delight and disbelief as the twin "Notches" rode our wave in tandem, gazing up at us with pleased recognition of what had just transpired. This experience with Notch did impact my belief that the dolphins can understand us. Yet, in spite of such strong evidence in the midst of this playful bow-riding experience, I was still not fully convinced.

Another joyful dolphin experience unexpectedly erupted out of the Gulf of California when hundreds of long-beaked common dolphins appeared out of nowhere to bound toward our boat with such a strong sense of glee that we exploded in applause. When this animated stampede of dolphins reached us, they made a sharp U-turn to the amazement and cheers of our group and then followed alongside our boat, as they each took cooperative and coordinated turns playing in our bow wave. After the last dolphin took his turn, he signed off—as dolphins do throughout the world—with an extra jump accompanied by a final glance and a chirp, as if to thank us for the gift of the wave and evoke one final moment of pleasure for our group.

The Irony and Play of Dolphins

After enjoying years of extensive diving with dolphins, the famed Jacques Cousteau concluded that they have a keen sense of irony—and I would have to agree. In fact, I also noticed during my decade with the dolphins that they relish in weaving a dash of irony into most of their interactions with humans by finding a way to add an element of surprise. They do this with impeccable timing by setting us up for one expectation and then startling us into laughter with a completely different result. Once they get us laughing about an unexpected twist, or screaming with surprise over an unforeseen outcome, our hearts get lighter and filled with joy as we become more relaxed, flexible, and easygoing.

One of the ways captive dolphins are able to hold onto their preferred role as tricksters in their more limited settings is to create opportunities to gain unexpected control over their trainers, even if only by refusing or delaying compliance, often while looking impishly into their eyes. Sometimes, they even manage to reverse roles with their trainers and assume the position of leader.

One dolphin named Keola regularly accomplished this feat by starting the Kahala Hotel's dolphin shows prematurely whenever their long-winded trainer was on duty. As this trainer stood with his back to the dolphins and droned on and on to his bored audiences about cetacean facts and stats, Keola would engage in a variety of antics behind the trainer's back that got the audience laughing. Whenever the trainer would turn to see what was going on behind him, Keola would stop, arousing even more laughter, and then begin again as soon as the trainer returned to his talk. Keola had found a way to employ classic pantomime humor to bring unexpected lightness and fun to this otherwise deadly boring situation.

A common trickster game wild dolphins enjoy is to taunt swimmers with their tireless delight in playing hide-and-seek. I have been teased many times by dolphins repeatedly jumping and dancing on the water's surface to lure our group into the water, then disappearing and going silent once we're in. When at last we give up and head for shore, the dolphins break into a loud chorus of chatter and squeals, revealing that they're right behind us, as if to promise that they're now reformed and ready to play. But when we turn back to join them, the dolphins fall silent again and cannot be found.

Sometimes this game goes on for hours, thoroughly exhausting the swimmers. Yet even though we're spent, we can't help but join the other duped swimmers in laughter at this exquisitely mischievous humor at our expense. Interestingly, this game invariably serves as a catalyst for the swimmers and beachgoers to become bonded through laughing as a group at each other and at themselves, which is a byproduct the dolphins seem to enjoy provoking.

Another game the dolphins take pleasure in playing is the leaf game, which they initiate by using leaves and fronds or some other debris, such as garbage bags or scarves, and other clothing they've found to exchange back and forth with each other or with us. They dive fairly deep with their object before dropping it and then look up at a designated swimmer to dive down after it. With each pass, the dolphin may take the object slightly deeper, typically challenging us to stretch ourselves a bit more. In other cases, they interject an unexpected element, either by not giving up the object after one of us has passed it to them or by letting it go and then scrambling to reclaim it before we have a chance to reach it.

This dolphin love of play constitutes a big part of their Higher Self persona, and because it's one that displaces discord with joy, it's a quality humanity would greatly benefit from assuming.

In addition to so much dolphin playfulness that I personally enjoyed, there are numerous Internet videos and photos memorializing them at play with others. These include clips of dolphins dashing among the whales with glee; frolicking with various domestic pets; or sneaking up to startle unsuspecting swimmers or surfers riding a wave.

Dolphins also appear to take extra delight in being photographed in as many settings as possible, and will not just hang out near the cameras in anticipation of a photo op, but will then eagerly play and pose for them once they start rolling. In fact, this response to cameras is so consistent that I often suggest newcomers swim near the photographers, since they're more likely to see dolphins that way.

This peeking and posing behavior, often preceded by sneaking up to startle the photographer, suggests that the dolphins understand their photo is being taken. This apparent understanding is consistent with their understanding of how mirrors and television work, as shown in multiple studies. It also reveals another aspect of the dolphins' love of fun and bringing cheer to the world.

A national television crew visiting Tonga benefited from this cetacean interest in being photographed when a pair of whales volunteered a ballet in front of their cameras. Even these seasoned photographers were awestruck by the wonder of the whales' unforeseen grace as they led each spin with their heads, followed by their bodies, with pectoral fins flowing behind in the style of a pirouetting ballerina.

Putting Play First

Initially, I found it hard to pull away from the piles of work on my desk to simply go frolic with the dolphins as they so often beckoned me to do. Yet each time I resisted going to the beach on a day when I felt called to play, I later discovered that something special had happened in my absence.

In order to remedy being left out of the fun, I decided to surrender more often to the dolphins' call to play. And whenever I did this I was surprised to discover that I was able to more easily, almost magically, finish my work with even greater ease than when I had skipped play to work. As a result, I was eventually able to see the error of my habit of striving to complete most or all of my work before allotting time for play. And the more I surrendered to play—and the laughter, fun, and joy that goes with it—the more I was reminded of the happiness of my youth, before work had become such an interruption to this vital part of life. But, of even more value, I noticed that my surrender to more play was augmenting my attractiveness in a manner that was drawing even more of my dreams to me.

I was beginning to grasp that by revealing their capacity for simple friendship and kindness, laced with the joy of humor and play, the dolphins were showing me a cluster of extraordinary gifts they possessed and that I too could have. But of even greater value, along with these gifts, it became clear during my struggle over whether to work or play that if I—and other members of my species—would embody the qualities of fun and play as fully as the dolphins do, our personal and collective lives would be transformed in surprisingly deep and magical ways.

Yet, in spite of the profundity of this lesson on the surprisingly magical power of play, there were even more dolphin gifts and lessons to come.

Put humor and play first on your agenda, for this is the source of the joy we work so hard to attain, while the dolphins simply play.

CHAPTER 5

Trait #3: Harmony among Themselves and with Others

Blending hearts leads to harmony.

ecause I was among the early pioneers to swim with dolphins in the wild, not enough people had gone before me to assure that I would be safe. As a result, I had no idea if the dolphins would be friendly and welcoming as I had hoped, or if they would behave aggressively toward me, as some had warned. I had read that dolphins are among the strongest of animals and that they are not only dominant over sharks, but are able to kill humans with a thrust of their tails if so inclined. I had also heard accounts of their aggression in captivity and of trainers who had been injured or even killed by ones who had changed their mood. In addition, I had learned from a number of reports that wild dolphins exposed to humans—particularly if fed by people trying to befriend them—may become uncharacteristically competitive and develop a taste for aggression. Thus, although I was counting on a friendly meeting between species, I had no assurance I would get one.

Harmony Delivered

Yet, in spite of my concerns, when the dolphins finally approached me, they did so in peace and in the context of harmony. I not only enjoyed this cordial first encounter, I also felt relieved. And because it went so well, I drove to Makua the following week in hopes of making a second connection, this time on my own, with these dolphins I no longer feared.

Upon my arrival I dove into the warm and what appeared to be the welcoming water of their beautiful beach. But, since I had only recently begun to swim there, I didn't realize that it didn't have a reef and could thus be subject to hidden currents and rough waves. So, I naively ventured out further than was wise, especially since I was swimming alone at an empty and unknown beach without a lifeguard.

When the sun unexpectedly went behind a cloud and changed the mood of the water, it got my attention and prompted me to notice that I had unwittingly ventured out about a hundred yards from shore. Realizing as a lifeguard myself that I was breaking all the rules, I nervously put my head down to swim as fast as I could back toward the beach. Then, seemingly out of nowhere I noticed loud, swooshing sounds coming from behind and toward me that were getting louder as they caught up to me. I had never heard sounds like these before and had absolutely no idea what could possibly be in the water behind me that appeared to be chasing me.

I felt instantly alarmed and swam even harder, as the sounds continued to gain on me. Then, just as I felt myself on the verge of a full-blown panic attack, about twelve large dolphins passed me on my left, less than four feet from my body, exhaling loudly and in unison as they passed. As I watched their large bodies rise up as a unit to loudly exhale and then slide back down just under the water's surface while swimming past me, I laughed aloud with relief.

I had not realized that dolphins start their mornings as a collective group, consciously breathing their way rhythmically into a meditative state. But, once I understood what these dolphins were doing, it made sense, and I later noticed them doing it on a few other occasions. I also noticed a small group of the lagoon dolphins—who had been captured when older and thus remembered the ways of the wild—starting their mornings with group breathing while swimming back and forth along the length of their lagoon.

Even though my first encounter with the dolphins had been friendly, after experiencing this collective power of their group breathing, I now felt appropriately subdued as an outsider in their world. Thus, when four dolphins approached me once I was closer to the beach and feeling safe again, I wisely remained passive and allowed them to take the lead, rather than swim toward them or initiate an activity of my own design.

Because I didn't chase these dolphins or move toward them from an angle, they had the opportunity to draw closer to me in their own time. As all four of them began to slowly circle around me, the largest male broke away from the others to draw even closer and to engage me in gazing. Then, due to some unseen yet viscerally felt signal, I knew to swim in slow motion, side-by-side and on a parallel course with this large, gentle being. The other three dolphins continued to swim along as well, but they remained in the background, while the large dolphin served as my guide. Following this encounter, I could always identify this dolphin by his essence, rather than his markings, and by the eye-to-eye contact and heart-to-heart connection he would reestablish between us each time we met.

Once connected, it felt as if I were receiving instructions from him on what to do next, which seemed to come from his entire being—his mind, his heart, his eyes, and even his body and skin. My years as a therapist helped me to listen in the sensitive, intuitive manner needed to grasp the quiet essence of his subtle, energetic instructions. Thus, the more I was still and listened carefully from my heart to what was happening between us, the clearer his communications became. As a result, I could feel this lead dolphin entrain to my movements and entrain me to his, as he firmly held heart and eye contact between us. It felt like a dance with a most enchanting partner, and I began to refer to this dolphin as my guide, since he seemed during this dance to be assuming the role of my primary instructor.

Meditative Harmony

As I swam alongside my new guide dolphin and his friends in this parallel manner, I could see and feel them shift incrementally down as a unit to a slower speed that seemed first to match the tempo of an eighth note, then a quarter note, and finally a half or whole note, as measured in music. These shifts down to a progressively slower cadence not only accommodated my slower swimming pace, but created the feeling that my brain was entraining to the calmer brains of the dolphins, taking me with them into a meditative state, similar to what I had experienced with the lagoon dolphins, but deeper. Interestingly, every time I subsequently swam with this foursome, they almost always pulled me into a similarly deep meditative state with them.

Ten years after noticing my own experience of being helped by the dolphins to achieve this deep meditative state, I came across a study in which people given an EEG to measure their brain waves after swimming with dolphins revealed similar results to mine. Not only did their brains register the slower alpha states, as expected, but they also recorded the even deeper theta states I had noticed feeling, similar to the soothing states of people in deep meditation.

Upon seeing these results, it occurred to me that the slower brainwave frequencies achieved in the presence of dolphins might also account for the deep levels of peace and harmony so many swimmers report feeling during and after swimming with these famously harmonious beings.

During my own periods of entrainment to the dolphins' peaceful harmony I was reminded of the times when I had spent long hours meditating on my own or during weekends with groups of experienced meditators. As I remembered how peaceful I felt during these periods of regular and prolonged meditation, it occurred to me that humans could rather easily achieve the same levels of harmony the dolphins enjoy if we spent more time in both individual and group meditation.

In support of this possibility, studies and scans show that time spent both in meditation and in the water with dolphins results in a notable reduction of anxiety and depression, along with newly unleashed feelings of well-being, not previously experienced.

The scans also reveal brain changes that result in people feeling calmer and more cooperative with others, similar to what we observe in cetaceans. I could actually feel my own brain mellowing out and positively changing during my decade in the water with dolphins and whales soothing my limbic system, and I find it fascinating that similar changes show up on the scans of experienced meditators.

The Harmony of Family Bonds

Although humans speak a great deal about the value of family, we often keep our children separate from our adult world by leaving them with a variety of caregivers or at school for most of their waking hours. Then during the time they have left to be with us, they are often left to spend much of it on their own, watching TV or using their other devices. As a result of this cultural norm, we not only miss out on special bonding time with our children, but many of them feel anxiously isolated and painfully alone, which is one of the primary causes of children behaving in disharmonious ways in their effort to soothe themselves or get our attention.

In contrast to our less cohesive and harmonious societal style, dolphins spend their days traveling and playing in groups together, while holding fins and caressing bodies. Their children are never left alone and appear to be strongly and happily connected to their families. Moreover, if one or two dolphins find a way to escape a fishing net, they tend not to leave unless the rest of their pod can also break free. Similarly, if a baby dolphin becomes trapped in a net, his mother will often attempt to enter the net to die with him.

The intensity of these bonds was highlighted during the United States Navy's sonar testing in Hawai'i's marine sanctuary in the spring of 1998, when researchers observed a large pod of dolphins all huddled together for support, vocalizing their angst in unison. Other observers watched helplessly for hours as they recorded a whale calf—separated from his mother and pod due to their disorientation when the sonar was on—breaching over two hundred times and pectoral-slapping over six hundred slaps before the sun set on his desperate effort to reconnect with his mother and pod. Since calf separation from family is rarely seen in cetacean populations, it was painful to watch this calf (and others who had been separated from their groups during these tests) struggling to cope in unfamiliar isolation. (See more on sonar testing in chapter 16, "What is the Sonar Problem and What Can we Do About It?")

We can see from these examples how important family bonds are to dolphins and why our capturing and separating them from their pods in the wild—and often again, once they're in captivity—is so agonizing for them.

This also explains why Iwa, the special healing dolphin, became so depressed after her move to a marine park that separated her from her firstborn son and the rest of the dolphin family she had adopted during her years at the Kahala Hotel lagoon. I happened to visit Iwa on the day before her transfer and learned from her trainer that she was pregnant. When I told Iwa aloud in front of my adult children that I would visit her and her baby at her new home, Iwa turned over and raised her white belly all the way to the surface of the lagoon, steadily gazing into my eyes. She remained there for several minutes, continuing to hold eye contact with me, as her belly flushed with pink. My children joined me in expressing amazement that she so clearly understood what I had just said and had responded with appreciation of my desire to stay connected to her and her unborn baby.

Reflecting back on that moment, I suspect Iwa's special response was in part meant to communicate to my own skeptical children that their mother's claims of communicating with the dolphins might not be so outlandish after all.

Many months later when I fulfilled my promise to visit Iwa and her baby, named Hoku, I found them in an extremely small and overcrowded cement tank, in shocking contrast to her spacious lagoon home. Iwa initially greeted me like her long lost hope and rushed to the side of the congested pool, where she stood upright before me in this honoring position while holding steady eye contact for most of my twenty-minute visit. When I asked aloud where her baby was, she quickly dove underwater, swam to the far end of the tank, and returned with her young calf, who also greeted me in the same upright position his mother was using.

The trainer who had let me into this back area and was observing us confessed her amazement as she watched Iwa do her best to both honor our bond and plead for my help in finding better conditions for her and her calf. Yet following this encounter and my inability to get Iwa moved, as I had foolishly promised during that visit, she refused to even look at me during subsequent visits, though I caught her stealing vacant glances from afar. It broke my heart to see this wonderfully loving and gifted healing dolphin exhibit such deep depression and a loss of hope for getting herself and her calf out of this abusive and humiliating arrangement and into better conditions. Iwa's plight served as one of the motivators for me to continue to write this book whenever I felt bogged down or challenged to pull it together.

Happily, years later, Iwa was selected to be the nursemaid to a young rescued dolphin who had been sent to the same park for rehabilitation. In order for Iwa to fulfill her duties, she was transferred out of her small tank to a larger one housing a group of other females she was able to befriend. Once Iwa's situation was improved, her depression lifted and she returned to greeting me fondly during my visits, until one day, she was no longer there. All inquiries as to where she had gone and why went unanswered, and all I could do was send her good wishes from afar—wherever she was.

Then, several years later, I traveled to the Big Island with my new and current husband, Tommy, to have lunch with an old friend of his at a hotel endowed with a large dolphin lagoon. While Tommy and his friend indulged in a post-lunch sundae, I ambled over to the lagoon to say hi to the dolphins. As I was attempting to commune with a group of adolescents completely uninterested in me, an older dolphin swam over to where I was standing and quickly locked me into a gaze that triggered my awareness that this dolphin was Iwa, though her spirit had been clearly broken by yet another break from her second adopted family.

After spending a while gazing at the subdued Iwa—and then introducing her to Tommy, who eventually joined me at the lagoon—I asked one of the trainers about the history of this dolphin. Fortunately, the trainer knew her story and was willing to inform me that her name was Iwa and that she had been sold to the hotel two years earlier. It anguished me to hear that Iwa had *again* been separated from her acquired family of female dolphins at the Oʻahu park, and I winced at how insensitive park owners and managers can be to the intense value dolphins place on family. It took me a while to let go and say goodbye to Iwa that day, since I knew this would be my last meeting with this wonderfully kind and healing dolphin—the first one to befriend and help me during *my* own separation and the ultimate breakup of my family.

Boundaries Support Societal Harmony

Bratty kids are no fun to be around and often inspire others to reject them. Yet in spite of this result, human parents are prone to tolerate their children's intrusive and off-putting behaviors, while cetaceans make it clear they won't abide the unpleasantness that goes with broken rules. Thus, rather than ignore crossed boundaries, as their human counterparts so often do, wild dolphins and whales use strong posturing gestures such as tail slapping, face-to-face head nodding, jaw clapping, or tooth raking of another dolphins' skin as a way to both convey and hold the line on their limits. Although these seem like rather tame warnings for such strong animals, their offspring know that if these lines are crossed, they'll be followed by consequences they would rather not endure.

I had once been duly intimidated by observing a group of dolphins slapping their tails on the surface of the water at a group of overzealous swimmers with a force strong enough to kill them if they didn't back off. I was also once approached with similarly aggressive posturing and head nodding by a large male, and though I didn't understand what I had done to offend him, rather than argue with the boundary he was setting for me, I quickly withdrew and left the water for the day.

Unfortunately, many swimmers fail to notice or understand these boundary-setting gestures and persist in pursuing the dolphins in spite of them. Both dolphins and whales generally show a great deal of patience and restraint with human rudeness, even when the humans are shamelessly overreaching their boundaries. But the cetaceans do have a limit. As a result, a number of aggressive people have been seriously hurt or even killed by cetaceans who eventually reacted to persistently invasive human behavior, much in the way the gentle and loving Jojo reacted to a man stuffing a cigar down his blowhole by killing him. Thus, although dolphins and whales are generally welcoming and friendly to humans, failing to heed their fair warnings to retreat is risky business.

To better understand the importance of not pushing against cetacean boundaries, it helps to be aware of the methods they use to dissuade their own children from daring to cross them, since these are the methods they are likely to use with us. For instance, they're known to prevent an unruly adolescent from breathing by holding him underwater for an extended period of time. They do this in order to reestablish their dominance and the parental authority needed to gain their offspring's full surrender to their rules without waging any further resistance or continued testing.

Although I don't advocate holding our children underwater to gain their surrender to our rules, it's critical to the harmony of our homes and world that we find some way to make our rules stick. Because the purpose of setting and holding boundaries is to create congenial homes and a harmonious society, allowing our rules to be broken is the primary error we make in our parenting and one that is preventing us from achieving either family or societal harmony.

Thus, while the cetaceans understand that holding to their boundaries is the key to creating a harmonious culture, we continue to struggle to grasp the importance of gaining clear surrender to our rules in our homes, our schools, and our society in general.

As a result, while cetaceans live in harmony with their families and others, humans are mired in the chaos created by a culture still wrestling with compliance to its rules. So, rather than allow our young to stay stuck in the trenches of resistance to our soft and wavy boundaries, we would be wise to learn from cetaceans how to hold more crisply and clearly to fairly set rules. We would also be wise to understand that just because we live in a culture lacking in clearly held rules, it's important to alter our own fuzzy standard when we enter the cetaceans' world, since they are likely to hold to their boundaries, even if our culture doesn't.

This clarity of cetacean boundaries was applied to a woman swimming in the ocean off the island of Maui. She initiated an overly forward approach to a pilot whale by moving into the space where he was resting and began to vigorously rub his back. The whale responded to this uninvited touch by taking the woman's ankle gently between his teeth, then pulling her about thirty feet underwater and holding her there until she thought she would drown. The whale then reversed course in the nick of time and nudged the woman back to the surface at the right speed for surfacing, where she gasped for breath at the last possible moment.

A video of this entire encounter—from intrusive touch to her gasping for air—(taken by her companion) went viral. Interestingly, it was met with cries about the dangerous nature of whales, rather than noting the clarity of this whale's boundaries and his willingness to hold them with the woman harassing him. I suggest that rather than fuss about the whale's method of teaching this woman to respect his boundaries, we would be wise to learn from him and his species about the importance of holding to the rules we've set if we want the kind of harmony and peace in our families, our schools, our society, and our world that the whales create in theirs.

Compassion Supports Harmony

Another way the dolphins share the harmony of their hearts with each other and the world is through their steady capacity for compassion. This capacity was demonstrated when a friend of mine took her three daughters to swim in the bay following her mother's unexpected and tragic death.

When she arrived she found a small group of dolphins gathered near the shore, seeming to be waiting for her group to arrive. When she and her girls entered the water, the dolphins encircled them in silence and swam a few feet from them for the full forty minutes they were there.

Equally poignant was the time our family went to the beach with a young adult relative who had recently and painfully become unexpectedly schizophrenic. The dolphins immediately surrounded and then circled this wonderful young man for the entire time he was in the ocean he loved and where he had spent his youth surfing and sailing.

In addition to offering humans so much compassion during their illnesses and periods of grieving, dolphins offer each other deep levels of caring and have been seen carrying sick or dying dolphins for days without stopping, until their assistance is no longer needed. Mother dolphins are also known to carry their dead calves along the surface anywhere from several hours to several days, accompanied by pod members who remain with the grieving mother for as long as she needs their comfort or until she feels ready to release her calf to the ocean or deposit it along the shallow shoreline.

It appears that in addition to cetaceans offering us their compassion, they seek ours as well, possibly to move our hearts to more caring and right action and the harmony that evolves out of those traits. This might be why a wild dolphin once showed me a propeller gash on his head; the reason why a lone captive dolphin shared the intensity of his pain with me and my adult children; why the smart and sweet Laukani showed me her red tongue in a cry for help; why Iwa conceded to show me her depression in the midst of her humiliation; and why so many dolphins bring us the plastic and garbage we've dumped into their home, the very plastic and garbage that's overwhelming and killing them.

It may even explain why stranding dolphins and whales take such great pains to swim to our beaches while in the midst of dying from exposure to our sonar in order to facilitate our awareness of what is happening to them.

And, finally, it seems that the orca mother who so famously carried her dead baby on her rostrum for close to three weeks for the world to see was not just expressing her own deep grief. It seems she was also forcing us to face what we're doing to the beautiful orcas with our abuses of them and their home—most recently by spewing newly increased levels of our military's lethal sonar into Puget Sound where they—and their salmon food source (also vulnerable to the sonar's force)—live. This mother's mixture of grief and rebuke gained worldwide attention and will hopefully evoke enough compassion from us to honestly address the boundless and unconscionable abuses we inflict on their world—and ours.

Protection and Rescue Enhance Harmony

In addition to offering generous doses of protection and rescue to each other, dolphins generously extend them to other species as well. My ex-husband, Tom, and I experienced this kindness when three dolphins were playing in the bow wave of our kayak. We were so distracted by our pleasure in sharing this experience with a friend who was enjoying her first dolphin encounters that we failed to notice we were gradually being pushed out to sea by a strengthening current, paired with a rising wind. Just as we noticed we were out too far and felt the wind at our backs picking up a notch, the dolphins abruptly dove underwater and left, as if releasing us to return to shore.

Even though our guest was not a strong paddler, she naively held onto the paddle I had asked her to hand off to me, impishly teaming up with Tom to get us back to shore, as if it were a game. Although I was surprised by her reckless behavior, I strove to remain a congenial hostess, as she and Tom paddled us toward shore at a standstill pace.

Then, quite unexpectedly, I felt a flash of alarm go through my body, and I no longer felt safe. Within moments, two large dolphins appeared, one on each side of our kayak, looking like solemn sentries preparing to escort us to shore. They were all business and swam in unison out ahead of our kayak, moving to the left of the course we were on, which I quickly realized was a shorter, more current-friendly path. Next, they circled back alongside our kayak to pick us up before swimming toward that part of the beach again. Their affect was one of gravity, rather than play, and our guest eventually picked up the shift in their mood from spirited to stern. Gratefully, she surrendered her paddle to me.

For the next half hour, we were barely able to inch our way toward the shore, as we paddled hard against increasingly strong currents and winds. I realized in the midst of our race against the elements that the dolphins were swimming by our side at a serious and steady pace as their way to encourage us to do the same. Once we were out of danger, I felt welcome relief and was finally able to exhale. Both dolphins leapt simultaneously out of the water, engaging me in a brief moment of eye contact before diving in unison deep into the water and out of sight. I was acutely aware that these dolphins had taken time out of their day to save our lives, and I sent them a message of deep gratitude and thanks.

I wasn't sure if my feelings of alarm had called these dolphins to our aid or if a signal from them had triggered my feeling of alarm—or if the two were interactive and simultaneous. In any case, I knew that I had been engaged in an intense nonverbal communication with the sentry dolphins, similar to the telepathic communications I had experienced with my own young children during times when they were in grave trouble and in urgent need of help. But the real key for me is that these dolphins had tuned in and cared, and in the process of saving our lives had established a strong bond of kindness and harmony between us.

The most dramatic rescue I've been personally involved with happened when a friend of mine encountered a problem with her scuba gear and couldn't breathe. After surfacing too quickly, she was not only paralyzed, but also found herself stranded and alone in shark-infested waters. While floating on her back, with only her arms to keep her limp lower body afloat in the choppy sea, she yearned intensely to be rescued and reunited with her young child, who was anxiously awaiting her delayed return to their boat. Before long, a group of dolphins arrived to circle her for the remainder of her ordeal, not only protecting her from the sharks, but also providing a calm presence that enabled her to persevere without panic until her rescuers arrived. In addition, the dolphins' ability to send out an energetic alarm, as they had done with me during our kayak experience, may have helped her rescuers to locate her.

But of even greater interest, the degree of her recovery from the bends, given the significant delay in her decompression treatment, was entirely unexpected and defied her doctor's prediction that she would never walk again.

In another modern cetacean rescue that took place in 2000, Elian Gonzalez, the Cuban child whose boat capsized while he was escaping with his divorced mother to the United States, captured our attention for several news cycles. Elian was known chiefly for the dramatic custody battle between his American family who was caring for him and his father in Cuba. But a sub-story that barely made the news involved Elian's dramatic rescue by a group of dolphins who cared enough about his fate to stay and help him throughout his ordeal.

During this period, I happened to be in direct contact with Cuban reporters from *The Miami Herald*—interested in the first edition of this book—who shared the details of this story with me. I learned from them that the first thing Elian told the fishermen who picked him up after his two days in the rough seas off Miami was that dolphins had circled the inner tube his mother had tied him into for the entire time he was in the ocean. They had also pushed him back up and into the tube whenever he had fallen asleep or started to slip through it. And, they had chased off the sharks circling the area, while constantly nudging his tube toward the shore. Six-year-old Elian was very certain that the dolphins had saved his life, which he shared with Dianne Sawyer during her interview with him on national TV.

Twelve adults—including Elian's mother—did not survive this ordeal, and the three besides Elian who did make it were hospitalized for a number of days for exposure, sunburn, trauma, and exhaustion. But this six-year-old did not suffer any of these physical or emotional problems—in spite of his double trauma of losing his mother and being in the rough seas on his own for two days. In fact, he was in such good shape at the time of his rescue that he was released from the hospital the next day.

As a trauma treatment specialist, I personally suspect the dolphins sent sonar pings to points on Elian's body, comparable to the tapping points used in the effective and popular Emotional Freedom Technique (EFT) trauma treatment protocol. (See Note #1 in the Notes section at the end of the book.)

The most recent dramatic rescue was offered early in 2018 to marine biologist and longtime whale researcher Nan Hauser, who was terrified that she might be killed by a nearly fifty-foot humpback whale who was repeatedly nudging and lifting her body while attempting to tuck her under his fin. Only later did she realize that he was protecting her from a large tiger shark swiftly heading in her direction.

Interestingly, a female companion whale, who had been tail-slapping at the shark throughout Hauser's rescue, approached Hauser's boat four days later on her birthday and began to repeatedly spy-hop—or lift her head out of the water—for several prolonged looks at Hauser. When Hauser accepted what seemed to her to be an invitation from this whale to enter the water, the whale positioned herself on her back four to five feet beneath Hauser and stretched out her pectorals to gently touch each side of Hauser's body in the gesture of a whale hug.

Some of Hauser's rescue was recorded on video and instantly went viral when she uploaded the footage a few months later. Interestingly, this veteran whale researcher of twenty-eight years had always strongly resisted all "anthropomorphizing" of whales prior to this experience, in order to stay within the required confines of scientific whale research. But she has since decided to include the attribute of altruism in her future studies of whales, which she no longer considers to be anthropomorphism. Not only did these whales win over her heart with their offer of harmony, but they also opened her mind.

The Harmony of Healing

Before swimming with the dolphins, I had read about their ability to generously help with human depression, autism, attention-deficit hyperactivity disorder, and autoimmune diseases, as well as with other physical and emotional problems. I initially assumed these claims to be excessive but later learned that a number of scientific studies validate them. Yet in spite of the consistency of these reports, the actual source of the dolphins' mood-elevating and physical healing skills continues to remain a mystery. I've always assumed that it comes from their ability to project their energy in a manner similar to the way Reiki or Qigong healers send energy from their own *chi* (*ki* - *qi*) to clients in need of more energy than they're able to muster for themselves.

This assumption seemed to be supported by Maka, following my attempt to send some energy to a gash on his chin that he had just shown me. In the midst of sending energy from both my heart and hands to his chin, I wondered if this was how the dolphins do their healing. I then considered taking a Reiki class to learn how to more strongly project my own chi energy, while I continued to send as much as I could muster to Maka.

As I pondered this idea, Maka slipped underwater and seemed to shoot a surge of energy into the lagoon, which caused a five-inch wave to rise up from out of the still lagoon about a foot in front of his head. This wave then moved rapidly—and visibly—through the water toward the pebbled shore on the other side of the lagoon about thirty-five feet away, where it snapped loudly enough against the rocks to make me jump and look in time to see the water splash about a foot into the air. I had witnessed these surges of energy-driven waves in the lagoon before, usually being pushed by a dolphin swimming about a foot behind them. But none of them had been shot rapidly across the lagoon, as Maka had just done, and I wondered if Maka had been tuning into my thoughts about how to send more energy. If so, he was not only showing me how to do it, but was also letting me know that dolphins are able to send a very strong shot of chi when desired.

The Harmony of Partnership Healing

When I first met Terry Pinney (*Dolphins: Angels in the Sea.* 1996) in Hawai‘i, she said that during a visit to a marine park prior to swimming with dolphins in the wild, she felt an urge to press her head against the plexiglass of a dolphin tank. After doing this, she noticed a vibrational sensation move through her head, neck, and shoulders. When she opened her eyes, she discovered that a dolphin was pressing his head against the partition from the other side.

Following that experience, Terry felt as though she had been opened psychically, and due to the accuracy of her new skills, she was invited by her local police to success-fully help locate a number of missing people and missing bodies. She also shared with me that Iwa worked in partner-ship with her to help heal the people she brought with her to the lagoon.

Although I was a student of metaphysics and had read a good deal about such possibilities, I was still highly skeptical of Terry's bold claims. Then one day, when I was alone at the hotel, peripherally watching the dol-phin show underway, Terry unexpectedly arrived on the scene. Iwa got very excited when she spotted Terry and behaved more exuberantly than I had previously seen. Terry felt no qualms about loudly imitating a dolphin chirp to communicate with Iwa, who was in the middle of her show, and Iwa responded in kind. Then, as the show con-tinued, Iwa kept her eyes riveted on Terry and added sev-eral extra jumps and wiggles to her routine, while Terry squealed and clapped in response. When the show ended, Iwa swam quickly over to Terry and warmly greeted her once again. Iwa then began to point her melon—or fore-head—toward the two autistic children Terry had brought for healing that day, and I felt myself finally being won over by Terry's claims of psychic connection and healing partnership with Iwa.

The Harmony of Shared Music

Researchers have found that wild dolphins and their whale cousins are strongly drawn to recorded music played into the water through hydrophones. They are even more interested in live music, ranging anywhere from my singing a song or toning OM into the water through my snorkel to quality music played by bona fide musicians. I have never been on a boat with live music aboard when dolphins and whales haven't shown up and stayed for as long as the music is playing.

As swimming with the dolphins became better known and increasingly popular, more and more people found their way to the dolphins' Makua Beach, including a young man who arrived with a large bongo drum that he set up in the sand. He then began to beat out a rousing rhythm on his drum, and just as I was noticing what a good drummer he was, dolphins appeared on the horizon and began from miles out to acknowledge his music by jumping and dancing their way toward shore. As the dolphins drew closer, the drummer beat faster and louder, while the humans on the beach and in the water found various ways to blend with the rhythm. When the dolphins arrived, they began to leap and spin their way between and around the gleeful swimmers. The drummer kept drumming, and the dolphins and people kept dancing, while our hearts were drawn rhythmically into the harmony of our shared music, dancing, laughter, and joy.

Canadian naturalist and professional musician, Jim Nollman, has both studied and enjoyed the harmony of playing interspecies music with the orcas on a more organized basis and has recorded his results, which can be heard on his website. The best known of these recordings, titled "Orcas Greatest Hits," demonstrates the orcas' enthusiasm for participating with human musicians, and at times even taking the musical lead.

Interspecies Harmony

In addition to creating harmony in their own environments and in their relationships with us, dolphins also extend play and kindness to other species, and have been seen twirling turtles, teasing eels, and snitching pelican feathers. They've also been observed kissing and nuzzling or playing with dogs and cats on piers as well as with family pets brought to visit or swim with them by boat owners. One dolphin aficionado reports going to Queensland to meet with some friendly dolphins in the area and, thinking his Rottweiler might pose a problem for the dolphins, decided to leave him in the car for the first few days. But the dolphins didn't show up until the third day, when he finally allowed his dog to join him, at which time the dolphins conspicuously befriended the Rottweiler first, before making friends with him.

My favorite image of interspecies harmony comes from the joy dolphins and whales find in each other. Whenever I've been on boats throughout the world in search of cetaceans, we've often encountered the dolphins and whales playing together. And, one of my friends was graced with the sight of a whale gliding beneath her boat with a dolphin hitching a ride on one of his outstretched pectorals.

Harmony with Nature and Aversion to Conflict

The real estate dolphins and whales select for their birthing nurseries and winter playgrounds are among the most beautiful in the world. They are usually comprised of ocean coves and bays stocked with an abundance of living corals, colorful fish, and an array of turtles and rays beneath the sea, while sunshine and sea birds fill the air. These location jewels tend to draw harmonious communities of wildlife and people living on the land encircling them. Yet, whenever disharmony erupts among these groups, the cetaceans are known to move to a different site, at least for the duration of the discord.

I experienced the truth of this during a summer when our dolphin-loving community felt agreeably connected, followed by a period when our harmony was broken. Although we were a diverse group of rich and poor, educated and unschooled, from the city and the country, we had bonded around our love for the dolphins. The dolphins—seemingly drawn to our harmony—would regularly show up to play for up to three hours or more.

That was the summer of 1995, and it was a wonderfully harmonious and happy time for us all. Then the gossiping began, and our group spilt into opposing factions.

Around the same time, a member of our group started a commercial venture of transporting tourists from Waikiki to swim with the Makua dolphins, but without teaching them how to do so in a respectful manner. As a result, instead of waiting for the dolphins to initiate an encounter, as we had been doing, the tourists aggressively pursued every dolphin who came up for air. In time, numerous kayaks were launched to help track down the escaping dolphins, followed by larger boats, some of which ran through the dolphins' pods at high speeds.

Before long, this agreeable beach had become a sad reflection of human disharmony and greed at its worst. Over time, the divisions between the people on the beach also deepened, and the dolphins made themselves increasingly scarce. Then, a drowning occurred, and the dolphins abruptly stopped coming to the beach. The tourists also stopped and the beach grew quiet.

In time, the dolphins returned for short visits, particularly on the days when we behaved kindly toward each other. Yet our encounters never fully returned to what they had been. And, though I missed our uniquely harmonious gatherings, I also felt blessed to have experienced what life can be when we hold onto our harmony in the midst of our differences, as the dolphins do. And so, achieving that quality—along with the other qualities of the Higher Self— became my new, most ardent goal.

The harmony of blended hearts coming together
for the good of all insures a loving, just,
and joyful world.

CHAPTER 6

Trait #4:
Exceptional Intelligence Used Wisely

Great scientists are not afraid of new frontiers.

—Margaret Mead

E ach of the dolphins' gifts of character is not only built on the gift before it, but reveals an evolving tapestry of the nature of dolphins. The fourth of these is the gift of exceptional intelligence used wisely.

Shocking Levels of Intelligence

I was surprised by the extraordinary demonstration of the dolphins' and whales' level of intelligence beyond anything I had anticipated. Yet, my discovery was met with skepticism whenever I shared it with others, due primarily to a long-term cultural assumption that views anyone perceiving higher levels of intelligence in other species as a victim of anthropomorphism—or a naive and flawed projection of human qualities onto others. As a result of this rebuke to those who believe in higher levels of conscious awareness and intelligence in other species—no matter how much of their brilliance the cetaceans manage to reveal—most of us feel cultural pressure to minimize or deny these revelations, lest we be viewed as unschooled or naive.

Yet, in spite of so much group pressure to deny the intelligence of other species, the reality is that cetacean brains are much larger and heavier than ours, with an extra lobe devoted just to emotion. Their brains also have more convolutions and folds than ours, allowing for additional housing of gray matter that forms extra pathways for the thinking and governing parts of their brains. These large areas of grey matter are also able to soothe the generally more reactive and less stable limbic system (including the highly alert and fear-patrolling amygdala), resulting in calmer, more cooperative and Higher Self behavior.

Cetaceans are also wired in a way that gives them the ability to communicate on multiple layers simultaneously and at auditory levels outside of our hearing range on both the high and low ends of the sound spectrum. Many of their trainers and others who've spent considerable time with them are confident that dolphins and whales are also telepathic. Yet, in spite of such strong support for their telepathic skills, there doesn't seem to be much interest on the part of our scientists in proving it.

This was made clear to me during one of my visits to Oʻahu's Sea Life Park when a trainer shared that their newly rescued dolphin—who had not yet learned their show's routine—had slipped out of his holding tank to join the others in their midday performance. Although all of the trainers were amazed that this new dolphin had executed the routine perfectly, when asked about doing research to see if he had done it telepathically, they showed no interest in investigating that topic, even though Sea Life Park is a research facility.

Research on Dolphin Telepathy

In addition to this standard reluctance to pursue research on dolphin telepathy, whenever research is conducted on this understudied topic it's often infected by the tenacity of our human superiority bias. For example, a dolphin named Lucky living at Sea-Arama Marineworld in Galveston, Texas, had been rescued from a fishing net at the age of four, and had thus been exposed to the full teachings and abilities of his family. Dolphin lovers Scott Jones and Jan Northup working at the facility hypothesized that all the dolphins in their care were telepathic and designed a study to test this ability in Lucky, the dolphin they considered to be the most aware and adept of their facility's dolphins.

In their study, Scott typed five instructions on separate sheets of paper and placed them in sealed envelopes. Jan, who did not know what instructions Scott had included in the envelopes, entered the tank area where Lucky was waiting. Two judges, who also had no knowledge of what the instructions said, were assigned to observe and record all of Lucky's behaviors.

Next, one of the judges rolled some dice to determine which envelope to hand to Jan first. Jan opened the designated envelope, read the instruction silently to herself, and mentally sent Lucky the message she had just read, without using any hand or other signals. This was repeated for each of the five envelopes.

Lucky was able to successfully execute the first two of these instructions but was unable to execute the third. Unknown to Scott when he wrote out the instructions, Lucky would not be able to accommodate the instruction to jump in this particular tank, since the roof over the top of it was too low to allow for a jump. Thus, rather than attempt the requested jump, Lucky sent a thought to Jan indicating he couldn't make the jump but would do something similar. When Jan received this message telepathically, she looked up and saw that the low roof would prevent the requested jump. She thus understood that Lucky was attempting to replicate a jump when he went to the center of the pool and bobbed up and down, raising his body fairly high out of the pool to resemble the first part of a jump.

For the fourth instruction, Lucky added a very dolphin-like element of surprise and nonconformance by performing the task before Jan had a chance to open the envelope and read the instructions. When Jan then opened the envelope, she was startled to find that Lucky had already correctly performed the task according to the instructions on her card.

Lucky then waited for Jan to open the fifth and final envelope and telepathically send him the instructions, before doing that task correctly as instructed.

When it came time to rate Lucky's performance, the judges marked his refused jump as a failure and the prematurely performed response as incorrect. Unfortunately, the limits of the research protocol required that the study conclude that Lucky was not telepathic, while ignoring his attempt to remedy the researchers' error on the third instruction and to show them his ability to know the fourth instruction prior to Jan's sending it to him.

I personally would love to know how Lucky was able to do it, and if he could do it on request, and I'm sorry the researchers closed up shop so quickly on this brief exploration into Lucky's telepathic skills. For anyone not bound by the limits of the research protocol, it's clear that Lucky was successful in demonstrating his ability to receive instructions telepathically. Lucky also intelligently took the initiative to correct an error in the experimental design, and also revealed an additional skill he possessed—that of knowing the fourth command before Jan did. This is a skill the researchers would not have known to study without Lucky taking the opportunity to reveal this ability. Yet, in spite of Lucky's efforts to show them what more he could do beyond what any of them had considered exploring, the researchers not only failed to pursue this ability, but lowered his score because of it.

Smart Enough to Act

Because very few studies are set up to test the outer limits of dolphin intelligence, much of what we know about their expanded abilities is a result of direct observation by people not involved in a study. I've personally had a number of these kinds of experiences while swimming in the wild with dolphins—many of them so dramatic that they would be hard for people to believe. But I've also had less dramatic and more easily believable indications of dolphin intelligence shown to me by captive dolphins, most of whom were older when captured and, like Lucky, embodied more of the natural intelligence and wisdom of their species.

One of these more enjoyable experiences occurred while sailing in the Bahamas with friends during a time when we chanced upon a sea pen holding two of the dolphins trained to play the role of "Flipper" in the sixties television series of the same name. Their caretaker explained that they were waiting to be sent to Cuba by their new owner in order to join the four other newly purchased Flipper actors he had previously sent. When our friends shared that I was writing a book on dolphins, the caretaker invited us to swim with the actors and then left to visit some friends.

We enjoyed an unusual hour of rambunctious and tiring play with these dolphins, who showed me an exhausting game, based on their strong telepathic skills, likely influenced by their famed trainer, Ric O'Barry, who trains his dolphins telepathically.

Because their play with me was so rigorous, I was too tired to pull myself out of their small sea pen and onto the platform several feet above my head. Tom, (still my husband at that time) pushed me from the water while my friends pulled from the platform, but the more attempts we made to get me out of the pen, the harder we all laughed. Finally, I fell back into the water, weak from hilarity, only to find one of the dolphins standing in an upright position beneath the surface, watching me with a wonderfully quizzical look on his face. When I looked back at him, our eyes met with a mutual twinkle, and he shook his head from side to side about eight times, while holding amused eye contact with me. I burst out laughing underwater, and he resumed shaking his head as I now choked on my laughter, not wanting to miss a moment of his look of humorous disdain.

Although he was a highly trained dolphin, skilled enough to play the role of Flipper and had likely been taught to shake his head in the negative, I was nevertheless struck by his selection of the perfect gesture for this situation. Because he was on his own in a sea pen, without trainers to select and reward his reaction to me, he was free to offer me his own wonderfully humorous and apropos response to my ungainliness.

Smart Enough for the Military

In stark contrast to my sweet Flipper friend, trained to entertain, the US Navy is in possession of what are probably some of the smartest dolphins in captivity, being trained primarily for warfare. The Navy has also done the most research and spent the most money on their approximately 130 dolphins, and has learned more than most about their intelligence. According to rumor, the Navy finds their dolphins to be so intelligent that they trust them to transport dangerously sensitive military hardware, serve as mine sweepers, and much more. But we will never know the full extent of what they've discovered, since most naval research is classified.

One revealing story that avoided the classified file was told to me by a civilian trainer, hired to help the Navy train their dolphins. It seems the Navy people had long since conceded that the dolphin sonar they were imitating was still more sophisticated than their own and that there was still more to learn from the dolphins about using sonar in the presence of enemies also possessing sonar. In an effort to upgrade their equipment to deal with such conditions, the Navy was running a number of tests to gain additional insights as to how the dolphins' sonar works.

According to the civilian dolphin trainer aboard a naval vessel during one of these exercises, two dolphins were asked to identify an object. But, when the dolphins attempted to perform the task, the Navy flooded the dolphins' sonar with a blast of naval sonar with the intent of scrambling the dolphins' sonar enough to interfere with their ability to read the image as requested. The dolphins quickly solved this problem, which the trainer deduced they had done by having one dolphin read the top half of the scrambled image, while the other read the bottom half and then joining both halves to see the full image.

When the naval personnel took their turn to identify the same object with their man-made sonar, the dolphins unexpectedly turned in unison to face the naval equipment and flood it with enough of their own natural sonar to disable it. This story not only reveals the high level of awareness the dolphins possess, but the wry humor that goes with their intelligence.

This kind of story, which periodically leaks from classified research into public awareness, coupled with the small sampling of non-military research done with dolphins, forces us to concede the truth of the claims made by aware trainers—and others—who've had regular contact with them.

The claim is that, at the very least, dolphins share the unique category of intelligence we previously believed only humans possessed. And, there's a good chance they possess even more.

What We've Learned from Observation

Interestingly, scientists conducting dolphin research frequently make their most dramatic discoveries about dolphin intelligence by observing the behaviors that dolphins voluntarily demonstrate outside the structure of research protocols.

One of these observations involved Tuffy—a dolphin working with the SEALAB II capsule project—who was being trained to rescue divers pretending to be in trouble. Once, after Tuffy had successfully performed one of these simulated rescues, the rescued diver had trouble opening his bag of fish, so rather than reward Tuffy for rescuing him, he waved him away. But Tuffy didn't move. Instead, he stared at the man in disbelief for a long moment before raising his flipper to gently bop the diver on the head.

This same dolphin later realized that one of the divers was actually in trouble and in need of genuine help; he responded quickly and went to the diver's aid in time to save his life. In another case, a dolphin being trained to assassinate was observed refusing to attack his target and was found instead resting his chin on the man's shoulder.

Yet, another dolphin named Kelly made the best of her situation after she was trained to clean her tank by bringing her trainer pieces of litter for a fish reward. When she found a good-sized piece of paper, she placed it under a rock, then tore off small pieces of it to take to her trainer one at a time, each in exchange for a fish. Kelly's design for getting more fish is consistent with research that has uncovered the ability of dolphins to problem-solve and design plans in ways similar to our own.

What We've Learned from Research

For years, most cetacean research had been ploddingly uncovering negligible aspects of the extent of dolphin intelligence by discovering things such as their ability to realize how mirrors and television work; their understanding of grammar; and, most importantly, yet not extensively pursued, their ability to communicate in spite of visual and sound barriers.

In the midst of these discoveries, it became clear that dolphins don't do as well with research protocols that require replication and often resist conforming to this component of scientific method, even when it means going without food rewards.

Yet, in spite of this resistance and its impact on dolphin research, Hawai'i's Dolphin Institute found a way to convince their dolphins to repeatedly respond to a command to do an original behavior in tandem with another dolphin. They accomplished this by asking the dolphins to perform their own original behaviors as well as the ones requested, which offered the dolphins enough variety to sustain their interest in the repetitive protocol.

Although the trainers couldn't explain how the dolphins were able to perform in tandem without the benefit of commands—and didn't set up a study that might help to explain it—people like me and others who've interacted extensively with dolphins outside of the parameters of research protocols believe this ability was due to their mixture of strong telepathic skills, their advanced intelligence, and their capacity for innovative problem-solving.

The Dolphins Reveal Surprising Levels of Intelligence

In the mid-1990s, the captive dolphins at Hawaiʻi's Sea Life Park and Research Center broke out of the narrow protocols and nominal peeks into cetacean intelligence that marine scientists were uncovering. They did this by surprising their trainers and the Park's science staff with a voluntary demonstration of their exceptional intelligence by showing them a much larger sample of their abilities than the trainers and scientists had even thought to pursue investigating.

They did this by watching themselves in the mirror placed in their tank as they blew all manner of bubbles, replicating structures and patterns found in quantum physics, a relatively recent breakthrough in science, first discovered by Max Planck in the early 1900s and later used by his friend Albert Einstein. This additional branch of physics has allowed progressive scientists to go beyond Newton's mechanical physics that explains the world we can see in order to also explain the invisible and more complex workings of the world we can't see. Observing the dolphins providing animated bubble diagrams of the basic elements of quantum physics blew the top off the question of whether or not the dolphins are intelligent.

During the same period when the Sea Life Park dolphins were creating their animated bubble diagrams to reveal some of the basic elements of quantum physics, a number of other cetaceans at other parks and in the wild were observed blowing similar bubbles. I was privileged to see many of these unique bubble designs blown by the captive Sea Life Park and lagoon dolphins as well as by the Hawaiian spinners at Makua Beach and on the Big Island. I was further blessed to see an array of bubbles blown by wild dolphins and whales in the open ocean during my travels to Australia, Tonga, Mexico, and the Bahamas.

These bubble structures appearing at multiple captive dolphin sites and in different parts of the open ocean at the same time that cetaceans were visiting with humans throughout the world begs the question of why these activities were appearing in concomitant clusters. Could it be that the cetaceans are joining forces to help humanity become a kinder, more conscious and loving species for our sake and theirs, and that they're using their ability to employ nonlocal and telepathic communication to work together on this shared goal?

Dr. Ken Marten, Director of Project Delphis at Hawai'i's EarthTrust, and his staff had the good fortune to study the bubbles blown by the Sea Life Park dolphins living at their research site. Dr. Marten published a clarifying article explaining the science behind the bubbles in *Scientific American* in August of 1996. (See Note #2.) Dr. Marten begins his unusual piece by declaring the bubble structures to be a phenomenon that would amaze any physicist and then proceeds to explain why, which I summarize for you here.

The bubbles blown by these dolphins, from both their mouths and blowholes, are not like typical bubbles that rise or break up in the water and dissipate quickly. Instead, they appear as smooth and silvery, stable rings of air, or as tiny to medium-sized round bubbles that linger in the water without rising or popping. The stability of these bubbles appears to be a result of the dolphins using their sonar to control and stabilize them in some way. Dr. Marten also notes that once the bubbles are formed, the dolphins play with them by swimming through them, biting at them, sucking them into their mouths and back out again like yo-yos, playing volleyball with the larger ones, or collapsing them into a cluster of smaller silver bubbles. The dolphins may also rearrange the shape of a ring bubble by turning it over on itself to create the sign of infinity, a double helix, or a number of other structures.

This bubble phenomenon was first noticed when two babies at Sea Life Park, alone in a tank without their parents, began to create their first bubbles. One of these babies was Tinkerbell, the daughter of the dominant female, Laka, who loved to share her bubbles with her appreciative trainer. Tinkerbell particularly enjoyed making the more complex spinning bubble rings, based on the design of a toroidal—or vortex ring—which some believe to be the energetic structure of our own bodies, brains, and hearts. This torus shape is also considered by many scientists and seekers such as Nassim Haramein, Bruce Lipton, and Gregg Braden to be the basis for all structures, from tiny spinning photons to the universe itself.

In addition to forming these universal structures, Tinkerbell also enjoyed demonstrating her ability to form ten- to fifteen-foot- long spiraling helices that looked like spinning helical DNA strands, which she then inserted into her toroidal rings. This favorite design of Tinkerbell's offers us an image suggesting that whatever is contained in our DNA (imbued with our chosen energies and attitudes) may be carried by the spin of our torroidals out into the world and beyond and then back to us again (after both giving and gathering information) on the return arc of the torroidal spin.

Not only were the vortex and helix shapes more complex, they were also interesting in view of the fact that the wild dolphins often acted out spiraling helix spins in front of me by twirling their bodies into these patterns. They would begin by gathering a group of dolphins together with their noses pointed downward, almost touching the sand. Then on some invisible cue, they would begin to rapidly spin and weave around each other's bodies, twisting themselves into a spinning braid traveling upward toward the surface in what looked like a double, triple, or quadruple helical DNA pattern. Then, when they were close to the surface, the dolphins would accelerate their spinning as they unbraided themselves into an explosion of energy moving upward toward the sky, but without breaking through the surface.

Interestingly, when this book was first published in 1999 under the title of *Listening to Wild Dolphins*, the quadruple helix DNA structure I saw the dolphins mimic the most often had not yet been identified, but was subsequently discovered in 2013 by a group of Cambridge researchers who hoped it might be of help in healing cancer. (See #3 in Notes.)

By engaging in these bubble-blowing and helix-spinning activities, are the dolphins using bubble ring and body movement 'drawings' of quantum patterns in nature to convey some meaningful information to us? If so, what might they be saying, and why? And how good are we at interpreting their messages?

Were the wild dolphins, who repeatedly showed me their quadruple spin in the late nineties showing me that the quadruple helix was on its way? Were the babies at Sea Life Park blowing bubble rings and vortices to show us diagrams of the structure of the universe made up of torus shapes? And what about the vortex rings that Tinkerbell fills with bubbles formed to look like helical DNA strands? Is she delivering a message similar to the one taught by the Stanford University-based Heartmath Institute, suggesting that our DNA—filled with our energies and urges—rides out on the vortices of our personal bubble rings into the universal field to plant our essence as well as our dreams?

Is she also showing us that our particular focus, whether on love or hate, not only impacts others, but brings back the outfall of that impact to us on the return spin. And, by showing us the path of our selected energies, is she—like the Heartmath Institute—helping us to understand that it behooves us to embody *only* the energies we want to have fill our own lives and world?

Scientists and seekers will understand these structures and messages far better than I do. But, it seems, at the very least, that the dolphins have successfully demonstrated that even their children are able to replicate patterns in fluid dynamics and quantum physics at a level well beyond the ability of most human adults. For those who want to see the dolphins' bubble rings in motion or images of the toroidal flow of our hearts and brains, and even the universe, there are ample sites on the Internet to explore, including those of Nassim Haramein, who has also swum with dolphins and is exploring and working to prove some of the same scientific impressions I received from them.

But, what else might the dolphins want to convey? Is it possible they have more information that could help us live our lives more kindly and with greater joy? If so, are we listening? Probably not. So, until that day comes, the dolphins will continue, as they always have, to find new avenues for getting through to us in their typically playful and unexpected ways, just as they did with Tommy in the following example.

Exposing High Intelligence During Play

As the first edition of this book was heading to press in 1999, it became increasingly clear that my long separation from my first husband, Tom, would soon end in a friendly divorce, and so it did.

Then, when Tommy and I ran into each other and began to date, I noticed early in our relationship that he was uniquely bright and logical, as well as a highly perceptive and insightful psychologist; yet he also had a strong preference for using a databased approach to understanding things. Although I'm also logical and like to ground my intuitive discoveries in science, I was not sure he would be comfortable with the extent of my sentient nature or my interest in things like quantum physics. Thus, in spite of being very drawn to him, I was also clear that I didn't want to spend my remaining years with someone uncomfortable with this aspect of myself. And so I made a point of revealing all of the many surreal experiences I had enjoyed with the dolphins, in order to test his comfort with someone like me.

One of the most phenomenal of my many unusual dolphin experiences was going into the water on days when they were in the water making their creaking, sonar sounds and then noticing through my mask that there were stacks of spinning miniature torus bubbles piled on the tops of each of my fingernails. These tiny bubble rings would remain on my nails for about thirty seconds or more before spinning away from my fingers out into the water and world beyond.

The bottom line is that they seemed to offer a diagram of the way our toroidals work—by spinning the essence of our personally selected focus—whether on love or hate—out into the world and then back to us on the return spin (after first collecting more of its likeness as well as its impact on others). I liked to think of these tiny bubbles as my own magic wands at the end of each finger, plump with the opportunity to select and send feelings of good will into the world (and beyond) and then pulling that goodness back to myself, multiplied.

I could see by the look on Tommy's face when I told him about the bubbles on my fingernails that I might have gone too far with my claims. But, it was the same look most people gave me—and the same look I would have given others sharing such events prior to my having the experience myself—so I didn't hold it against him.

Nor did I go so far as to share with him the multiple demonstrations of sonoluminescence in the form of beautiful blue bubbles suspended in the water before my eyes (that I assume the dolphins were bombarding with their sonar). Neither did I share the one possible demonstration of cold fusion in which bubbles that seemed to be boiling appeared on the surface of the water right in front of me. But, I share them here for the sake of scientists and others who might understand what these events mean and how to capitalize on their potential use for good. (See Note #4.)

Then to my surprise, on Tommy's and my first day of swimming together with the spinner dolphins at Makua Beach, the moment he dove into the water, a stack of these bubbles appeared on each of his fingernails. The expression on his face was priceless. He's a multiple time participant of the arduous Molokai canoe-paddling race; he has swum and surfed in Hawaiian waters his entire life; yet he had never seen anything like that before. He tested and retested this reality a couple of times, while the dolphins kept the bubbles coming—but it didn't take long before he was convinced. He then looked over at me and grinned from ear to ear, pointing with delight to his bubbles.

By giving this reality-based data lover his own experience of such a surreal phenomenon, the dolphins had found a swift and playful way to add credibility to my claims.

That day of like-minded bonding between Tommy and me also paved the way to our engagement a few months later. And when I treated him and one of his daughters and granddaughters on his birthday to go with me on a boat to swim with the dolphins, he was amazed that a group of females with their babies were waiting at the dock to greet us before our day with them even got started.

There is enough research on dolphins, coupled with my own direct observations and those of others to support the proposition that both captive and wild dolphins are highly intelligent beings who use a complex system of linguistic sounds and sonar imaging skills for multiple purposes. There is also replicable evidence that they are telepathic, in addition to there being strong support for the notion that they have at least some understanding of fluid dynamics and quantum physics. Yet, in spite of these findings, humans continue to question and probe their most basic levels of intelligence, and some even continue to question whether or not they possess language.

Given this backdrop of human reluctance to honor either the intelligence or the language of dolphins, I was startled by a most unusual and surreal communication the dolphins initiated with me one day as I sat on the warm golden sand surrounding their beach. I share this story in the following chapter.

The question isn't whether or not the dolphins can talk, but whether or not we are listening. Once we begin to listen, a wonderful new world will be revealed.

CHAPTER 7

Trait #5: How Telepathy Serves Truth and Clarity

We can achieve clarity only by being fully naked before others about who we truly are.

The gift of telepathic communication was delivered to me by my dolphin friends much in the way a surprise party is presented, a bit shocking at first, but then evolving into a source of great joy.

Because telepathy is a direct method of delivering mind-to-mind and heart-to-heart communication, it enables us to receive the truth of what others are thinking and feeling without the encumbrance of verbal translation and the potential for misinterpretation. But even more important, when in the presence of others who are telepathic, hiding our thoughts is no longer possible, which forces us to first fully face our own truths and to then share them openly with others.

The Surprising Value of Telepathy

Learning to be fully transparent while spending time in the dolphins' seamless and telepathic world inspired me to voluntarily practice this same level of transparency while on my own or when immersed in my own non-telepathic society. Interestingly, practicing this new level of full transparency with myself and others not only enhanced my personality and life, it also brought me into better alignment with my Higher Self and the person I most want to be.

Although it took me a long time to fully accept that telepathy is real and that the dolphins and I were truly communicating in this fluid and open manner, one interaction after another made it impossible for me to continue to doubt it, and I finally surrendered to its reality. With this surrender, I also surrendered to what the dolphins were saying and the potential of their messages for helping me personally and our society in general. The collection of incidents I share in this chapter worked together to finally bring me to this understanding.

First Telepathic Transmissions

Swimming with dolphins had become a regular activity for me throughout the 1990s, and each connection revealed a bit more about the conscious nature of these highly intelligent beings. Then, after a year of enjoying our time together, something happened that completely altered my view of dolphins. And, with this alteration, my view of the world was also dramatically changed.

I was sitting on the dolphins' beach reading a book when I felt strongly drawn to look through my binoculars at the horizon, where I noticed a group of dolphins journeying westward. I watched them swim in this direction for about twenty feet before diving in unison and then surfacing a few feet ahead of the spot where they had dived. The dolphins then swam another twenty feet before diving in unison again and then surfacing a few feet ahead of that new spot—and so on.

Suddenly, my idle observation of the dolphins' rhythmic path was interrupted by an unexpected notion that they would not continue in this direction and that I would need to move my binoculars eastward to pick them up again. This made no sense, but I responded to the idea, since it had registered so strongly in my mind.

As I then focused my binoculars on an eastward point along the horizon, I was startled when a dolphin jumped into my sight. Following this jump, a second impulse told me to reverse my binoculars again and look about twenty yards to the west. Once again, I complied with this odd prompting and found another dolphin jumping into my sight. A shiver ran through my body as a third impulse pointed me in the direction of where the dolphins might be. Once more, my hunch was correct, and the dolphins rewarded me with another jump.

This activity continued for what seemed like fifteen minutes or so, as I successfully tracked the dolphins multiple times with only two incorrect responses. During this period, I slowly accepted the notion that the dolphins were the ones sending me these impulses and rewarding me for my correct responses with their jumps. Once this was understood between us, they dove and didn't resurface, a behavior typical of wild dolphins anytime they have completed an interaction with someone.

As I put my binoculars away, it occurred to me that the dolphins had sent their thoughts to me much in the way a martial arts master sends the energy of his chi in the direction of his opponent to knock him off balance. It was also similar to the way dolphins send the energy of their sonar out ahead of them to click on things, including me and others in the water with them, or to stun fish. In fact, previously experiencing the dolphins' sonar as a light, pulsing ping or tapping sensation on my skin had made me aware that they had the ability to project their energy through the water to wherever I was located—even when there was a good distance between us.

But in this case, it felt as though their ideas—rather than their pings—had been sent forth and impressed upon my mind, allowing their thinking to penetrate my awareness. I also noticed that their ideas felt quite different from my own thoughts, just as the ideas I receive from a radio are clearly separate and distinct from mine.

As I slowly absorbed the possibility that the dolphins were transmitting their ideas to me, something even more startling happened.

The Dolphin Garden

My experience with the binoculars happened at a time when I was still married to my first husband, Tom, who was at the beach with me that day. He had just emerged from the water to join me on the beach and suggested we take the kayak out. As soon as we were comfortably launched and in the process of finding our paddling stride, my guide dolphin began to send loud, high-pitched sounds in our direction. The sounds were such that they uncharacteristically moved out of the water and into the air where we could hear them while sitting in the kayak.

Although I couldn't see this dolphin, I turned my face toward what seemed to be the origin of his sounds and chirped back at him, and he responded in kind. We continued to exchange chirps back and forth in this manner as Tom and I followed his sound out toward the horizon to a much deeper part of the ocean. Suddenly, my guide dolphin got quiet, and as we looked for where he had gone, he surfaced so close to our kayak that we both startled and had to stop paddling in order to avoid hitting him.

He remained very still in this position beside me and looked directly into my eyes, evoking in me a strong urge to drop down to my heart, as I often do with pets and children or my clients, in order to more fully hear their silent messages. Once in my heart, I could clearly sense my dolphin guide's message and realized he was telepathically inviting me to join him in the water. It felt as though I was being asked to join in the dancing at an important event, and I began to fumble for my fins and mask as he patiently waited for me to get assembled and into the water. He then mentally invited me to perform shallow dives with him, which I did for several minutes until he slowly swam away from me and out of my sight, while maintaining voice contact between us.

Next, I received a message to look down, and when I did, I saw what looked like a magical garden filled with about five robust dolphins directly below me, all larger than the ones I was accustomed to seeing in the shallower part of the beach. I felt like Alice in a wonderland of oversized dolphins swimming actively all around and under me, filling me simultaneously with fear and wonder. In an instant, I had entered a fantasyland and was trying to process exactly what was happening—but whatever it was, it felt as if my encounters with the dolphins were getting "curiouser and curiouser."

Meanwhile, these sturdy dolphins began to swim by me in twos and threes as if in a promenade, and in spite of my fear of their larger size and unfamiliarity, I cooed in response as each grouping appeared before me. Next, a group of four of these large dolphins gathered right below me and started to spin in the helix formation as described earlier, and I felt increasingly fearful as their massive, spiraling energy moved upward toward me. But to my relief, they broke out of their spin with an explosive burst of power just before hitting me.

Several of them circled back to offer me eye contact, while assuring me that their explosion of energy had been a gift, not a threat. A few more joined the circle, which now included my guide dolphin, and I felt my heart expand to accommodate this new level of enchantment. Then the dolphins left, and I've never seen them since—adding to the dreamlike quality of the experience.

As I scrambled back onto the kayak, I asked Tom if he had seen what happened. He said he had seen it and was surprised by the size of this group of dolphins. I felt grateful for a witness to this surreal experience, and I slipped into a dreamy state as he paddled us back to shore. When we arrived, I felt a compulsion to write, so I sat on the beach scribbling an account of this mind-altering experience on a few scraps of paper. In that moment, *Compelling Conversations with Wild Dolphins and Whales* was born.

By the end of the day, my perception of dolphins had completely shifted from seeing them as friendly and fascinating animals to viewing them as fully sentient beings, not only able to communicate telepathically but also as purveyors of new horizons of experience and knowledge.

Upon returning home from the beach, I felt a strong urge to sleep that wouldn't be denied, so I surrendered to a narcoleptic-like nap. As soon as I had crawled into my bed, my body began to vibrate gently from within, as if I were purring. It was a strange yet pleasant sensation that initially scared me, but that I was able to eventually embrace as I relaxed and fell into a deep sleep. When I awakened, the vibrating had stopped, but a feeling of bliss lingered within me for the rest of the week, followed by my heart opening more to others. (See Note #5).

As I attended to my various activities over the next few days, I felt my heart open with a desire to send love to everyone I passed in the same way the large dolphins had done with me. And so during the next days and weeks, I viewed everyone who crossed my path as a highly valued being and felt a strong urge to send love to each one of them. In time I realized that my special encounter with the large dolphins had opened up this new place of caring in my heart, and I felt grateful for these freshly awakened and fuller feelings of love for others.

Yet in spite of the positive impact my various dolphin encounters were having on me, they persisted in feeling surreal. Thus, I strove over the next few years to seek more understanding and proof of the telepathic communication and exceptional experiences I was having with the dolphins.

I began by reading all I could about the nature of telepathic and intuitive listening and how to engage in using it. I was delighted to discover that shifting my awareness to my heart in order to "listen" from that place of deep compassion in me—as I had done over the years with children and clients—was the key.

The more I consciously did this both inside and outside of my therapy practice, the more I was able to intuitively hear the truth of others and the more sensitive I became. Not surprisingly, I also became a better therapist as I honed my ability to listen more deeply—and at times telepathically— to my clients and to the children in my life (including my own, my clients', and the ones attending the preschool I had been a part of developing). The better I got at listening in this deeper, more intuitive manner, the more fully my clients felt heard and at times would get tearful in response to being so deeply understood.

Of equal, if not more, importance is the breadth of comprehension the art of telepathy offers, which not only helps to bypass misunderstandings, but also prevents dangerous secrets and hidden agendas from undermining our relationships and world. Once I grasped the enormity of these benefits, I began to study telepathy with renewed zest, starting with confirming once and for all whether or not the dolphins and I were truly engaged in it.

Telepathy as an Aspect of Dolphin Communication

After my day of sitting on the beach with my binoculars while interpreting the dolphins' transmitted thoughts, I paid more attention to what the dolphins were saying and the way they responded to my messages in return. By sharpening my observations, I hoped to either confirm or deny that they had made a clear and deliberate telepathic connection with me.

Once I committed to testing this reality, the dolphins seemed to become actively engaged in helping me confirm the validity of the telepathy between us. They not only assisted by using even more ways to demonstrate their ability to understand me, but by also reinforcing me whenever I correctly understood them.

Yet even as they cooperated with my desire for proof, they did so in the context of their own personalities, rather than mine. Consequently, their confirmations always contained an element of humor, expressed with delays, surprise, or a bit of joy as they rewarded my correct responses or acted out their understanding of something between us. These assurances made it seem as though we were engaged in an ongoing and playful game of charades. And though it was more fun and interesting to do it their way, I had to stay open and alert in order to understand the variety of ways they were communicating with me.

This happened one day when I was swimming in the shallow part of Makua Beach at a time when the dolphins weren't there. I felt even more moved than usual by the ocean's beauty and began to hum softly into my snorkel, "He's got the whole world in his hands." Within a few minutes, about thirty dolphins unexpectedly drew near and swam beneath me in extra-slow motion. As I continued to sing, a pair swimming directly below me caught my attention, due to their unusual looking, precisely side-by-side position to each other, rather than in their usual formation of one slightly ahead to provide a slipstream for a friend following a bit behind.

As I studied them more closely to see what they were doing, I noticed that all of the dolphins swimming below me were doing the same thing in order to accommodate the fact that they had their flippers hooked together. As I puzzled over this behavior, the dolphins right below me unhooked their flippers in slow motion and then moved them meticulously back together again, in order to reconnect them in a manner I would be sure to notice.

With delayed recognition, I exclaimed in my mind, "Oh my God, are you holding hands?" With this, the pair below me repeated their unhooking and re-hooking gesture and then looked at me deliberately, as I laughed in acknowledgment of their acting out the words of my song.

My Search for Proof

Because an open acceptance of telepathy is generally rejected in our culture, those who believe in it are for the most part ridiculed. As a result of my being infected by this strong cultural bias, no matter how clearly or how often the dolphins rewarded me for understanding their telepathic transmissions, I continued to struggle over whether or not I was actually talking to another species or was lost in the zany world of Dr. Dolittle. To put my question to rest, I turned to collecting more research, along with the anecdotal experiences of others.

In my search I discovered that although most dolphinarium managers require their trainers to discount telepathy, many of the best and most longstanding trainers break through this barrier and adopt a firm belief in the telepathic abilities of dolphins. Ric O'Barry, trainer of the six dolphin actors who played the role of Flipper, is the most famous of the trainers who believes in their telepathic skills. And, even before I had read about O'Barry's use of telepathy while training his dolphins, I had noticed that the Flipper actors he trained were communicating with me telepathically during our swim together in the Bahamas.

Ric O'Barry's views about telepathy began when the dolphins he was training performed a trick correctly before he had given them their command. This was particularly interesting because the first time they preempted O'Barry's instructions was on a day when he was planning to request that they do their tricks out of their usual order. It was as if the dolphins had telepathically read his mind and wanted to utilize the planned changeup to show him they already knew about his scheme before he had a chance to use it.

Dean Bernal, longtime friend of the most famous wild, sociable dolphin, Jojo, is absolutely certain that Jojo, as well as the other dolphins he's met throughout the world, communicate with him telepathically. I was blessed to meet Dean in person and not only hear his array of stories confirming telepathy, but to also converse with him extensively on this topic of fascination to us both.

Frank Robson, one of the early dolphin trainers at Marineland in Ontario, Canada, and author of *Pictures in the Dolphin Mind* (1988), believed so deeply in dolphin telepathy that he used only mental images in his training program, while rejecting all use of whistles or food rewards. He believes the dolphins responded to the requests he formed in his mind simply because they liked to please him. In addition to his telepathic relationship with the captive dolphins he trained, Robson befriended a group of wild dolphins who also responded to the mental pictures he sent to them. Interestingly, one of these dolphins named Horace could even sense when Robson's group planned to take their boat out and would dash to the place they had decided to go, getting there ahead of them and then waiting for Robson's group to arrive.

Robson views all dolphins, both captive and free, as highly telepathic and advises humans wanting to communicate with them through this medium to approach with a good heart and a sincere desire to listen. He also advises humans to let the dolphins take the lead, rather than give them commands similar to ones they've seen in shows, since dolphins don't like to be bossed—and when their ability to eat doesn't depend on you, they're unlikely to conform to such directives.

Yet I find that even when you're not being bossy, most dolphins would still rather tease than conform. As a result, they may—or may not—give you what you want, but only after you've released any notion that they'll respond on your terms or your timetable.

The Origins of Telepathy

I also learned in my search that telepathy is a natural state enjoyed between two beings, in which both are able to send and receive each other's thoughts (and feelings) without the need for or the encumbrance of audible words. Telepathy is used regularly in many indigenous cultures as well as in our own culture with preverbal children—and it can be used with animals and nature whenever we tune into their world. It's also well known that many identical twins are able to communicate telepathically, which results in close bonds and open channels of communication between them. A basic understanding of telepathy explains why people may realize a family member is calling them, even before the phone rings; why people may think of an old friend a few hours before running into him or her; or why people may know when someone they love is in trouble, sick, or dying.

Yet in spite of the comprehensive nature of telepathic sharing of information, we view verbal interactions as the zenith of communication and consider early verbal language in our children to be a sign of intelligence. However, if we pause to reflect, not only does verbal communication allow room for misunderstandings and deceit, but the concrete nature of it is also more cumbersome. As a result, verbal communication is less able than a telepathic transfer of information to share the breadth of our thoughts and feelings with others.

The truth of this was brought to my awareness when my son, his wife, and I were observing a distressed dolphin obsessively twirl in circles upside down over the floor drain of his small tank. After watching spellbound for several minutes, the three of us—two psychologists and a clinical social worker—commented on how helpless we felt, as our hearts went out to this troubled dolphin. The moment we expressed our concern for him, the dolphin pulled out of his twirling and swam rapidly toward us, looking very much like a torpedo, as dolphins do when they swim at us in this straightforward manner.

Confused by this sudden change in his behavior, we all fell silent as we watched him approach us. He stopped within an inch of the glass separating his world from ours, looked deeply and directly into our eyes, lowered his head with the top of his melon aimed at us, and then paused in this position before us. Within moments, all three of us began to cry, and my sensitive daughter-in-law ran in confusion from the area. When my son and I caught up with her, we each shared that we had viscerally felt the intensity of the dolphin's pain within ourselves rather than being objective, albeit compassionate observers.

It seems this dolphin had transmitted the full experience of his unremitting feelings of loneliness, boredom, sadness, and hurt to us—much like he might send his sonar pings into the world. As a result, information about this dolphin's imprisonment in his painfully small pool penetrated us at a depth impossible to glean in the course of human conversation.

That moment not only provided further confirmation of how dolphins communicate, but also gave us a complete and personal account of what it would be like to experience endless moments of captivity. Even though I had read well-written accounts of the agony of imprisonment, it wasn't until I actually felt this dolphin's torment within my own being that I gained a more personal and expansive understanding of how challenging it is to experience captivity minute by minute, day after day, and year after year. Put simply, it felt unendurable.

Not only was it impossible to misinterpret this multi-layered message, our knowledge of his pain and feelings of compassion were intensified. I could see how this form of communication would not only challenge a society to be more honest, open, and real, but to also be more compassionate and caring. And I could see how much it would sensitize us to our oneness and commonality, along with the need to treat everyone fairly.

Telepathy at Work

Because telepathy seems to work similarly to a two-way radio or fax machine, communication can take place anytime two or more parties who believe transmission is possible tune in simultaneously to each other. Sometimes dolphins tune into our conversations when we are least expecting it, but if we tune into them as well during these periods, communication is established.

For example, when I was visiting our local marine park, a trainer told me about Laukani's mysterious health problems, including the fact that she was so weak that one of the other dolphins always swam in front of her to provide her with a slipstream for drafting. As we were discussing the rest of her symptoms, Laukani positioned herself directly in front of us and remained there throughout our conversation, holding steady eye contact with me the entire time to let me know she wanted to join the conversation.

I suggested to the trainer that Laukahi, who had been on antibiotics for years, might have candidiasis, since she had the classic symptoms of a long-term fungal infection. Then, in an effort to confirm my suspicions, I asked the trainer if Laukani had symptoms of thrush in her mouth. With that, Laukani opened her mouth wide and held it open for several minutes while I closely inspected to see what she was showing me. She did, indeed, have swollen red gums and a bright red ring around the edges of her tongue. It was clear this dolphin knew that I had asked about her mouth and wanted me to see it. There was no trickster here; the usually playful Laukani was serious, and I assumed she was cooperating in hopes of getting help.

Although the trainer didn't believe in telepathy, she could clearly see the blazing inflammation in Laukani's mouth. So she ignored the method of Laukani's communication and shared this information with other staff members, along with the idea I had promoted that her problem was likely fungal. Fortunately, the other staff members agreed to put Laukani on antifungal medication, which dramatically cleared up her symptoms and improved her health.

During my subsequent visits to the park, Laukani was always the first to greet me, often standing upright before me in an honoring way. She would then gaze at me throughout my visit. It seemed clear that she was grateful for my understanding of her message at a level most humans dependent on verbal communication wouldn't have fully grasped.

Once I learned to respect and tune in to the dolphins' telepathic conversations, I sometimes awakened in the morning and sensed a call to visit them at the beach. Each time I responded to one of these calls, no matter what time I arrived at the beach, the dolphins were in the center of it, jumping to greet me. I also noticed that any ideas or pictures that had passed through my mind of what would take place with them that day usually materialized.

For example, the first day I thought of taking my camera to get some photographs for this book, I received the message that the dolphins would show me their jumps only after I put my camera down. I thought this was an odd communication, and assuming I had mixed up the message or imagined it, I simply dismissed it and took off for the beach with my camera in tow. As I was looking for a place to park, the dolphins sent me a suggestion to meet them at the cliff, where I had enjoyed some of my most interesting times with them. Prior to my awareness of the possibility of telepathy, I would have ignored this thought flowing through my head and remained at the beach. But now that I was paying attention and responding to the ideas in my head, I headed for the cliff, which was adjacent to the beach.

As I parked, I noticed that the dolphins were already there and seemed particularly frisky. Several executed high leaps, broad jumps, and a rare backflip before I could even get out of my car. I quickly gathered my gear together and set up my beach chair and camera in hopes of capturing these special shots. But once I was prepared, the jumps ceased abruptly and the dolphins remained silently beneath the water. I sat for a long time with my camera set and poised, waiting for a surprise jump. But none came, and the water remained unusually still.

Eventually, I assumed the dolphins had left the area, since they weren't even coming up for air, so I relaxed and rested the camera in my lap. The moment I did this, the leaps began again. When I picked up my camera, the activity ceased. I soon realized I was being teased and began to chuckle. This went on for another twenty minutes before I remembered that this game had been foretold earlier that morning.

The consistency of this playful game and the dolphins' tenacious teasing got me laughing aloud, as I pleaded for at least one shot. Although I didn't get a single picture, I drove home with a big smile on my face. I had gone to visit the dolphins in spite of a busy schedule that day because I had been feeling a bit low, and I left filled with endorphins and a parting message from the dolphins that my elevated mood was more important than the photos. They were teaching me to be more dolphin-like and playful, rather than serious and goal-oriented, as humans like me are prone to be.

This became a consistent message delivered to me from the dolphins in a variety of ways, and they would often send me home laughing and joyful, in lieu of helping me to meet my goals—even when my projects often included helping them in some way.

A week later, I felt pulled to the cliff again, and when I arrived, twenty dolphins were gathered at its base, quietly bobbing up and down. Once I was settled into my beach chair with my camera poised, the dolphins began to jump and play, so I tried to capture some shots of them. Then, just as I noticed how hard it was to see a jump, aim the camera, and capture a picture in focus, I received a message to simply point the camera at a place on the water, and the dolphins would jump into my sight, just as they had done with my binoculars a few years before. I was skeptical and assumed I had made up this idea, but I tried it anyway. When I then pointed my camera randomly at a spot on the surface of the ocean, a dolphin leaped into my sight. When I tried it again, the same thing happened, so I continued to point my camera at spots where I felt called to point it and was able to capture about fifteen dolphin jumps on film.

Next, I began to wonder how I would get a shot of the high leap I envisioned for my book cover. Almost immediately, a dolphin leaped twenty feet into the air right in front of me, portraying the image of the cover I had in my mind. Prior to this, I had seen dolphins jump this high in the open ocean on only a few rare occasions, so I sat stunned for a while, absorbing the profundity of this communication between us. Unfortunately, it happened so quickly that I failed to capture the dolphin's perfect cover jump on film.

On a boat trip several months later, I was telepathically reminded of this technique for photographing dolphin jumps and was able to capture a few truly good shots. That same day, a young dolphin kept waving his tail at one of our guests, who was disdainfully amused by my belief in dolphin telepathy. Every time I mentioned an apparent connection between our friend and the young dolphin waving his tail at him, the dolphin would vigorously wave his tail again until he got us all laughing—including our guest, who eventually surrendered to the possibility that he might be the focus of a telepathic interaction.

Taking any one of these events in isolation would not cause many people to conclude that dolphins are telepathic, but when this small sampling of my larger collection of stories is lumped together, it becomes a challenge to hold firmly to the idea that dolphins do not possess this ability. The reason that trusting in their possession of this skill is so important to an understanding of dolphins is this: The unmasked communication telepathy affords the dolphins rests at the heart of their open and transparent society. And it's this transparency that impels the dolphins toward their very best selves and full alignment with the purity of their souls.

Yet in spite of so much proof of the validity of the dolphins' telepathic skills, I continued to want more, especially since telepathy has been so disparaged in my own society that even when I repeatedly experienced it, I had trouble believing in its truth. And, like Alice in Wonderland, I felt a need for additional reassurances that the world before me was real.

Reinforcing Bubbles

Even though telepathic interactions with the dolphins continued to occur on a regular basis, I persisted in questioning their veracity. Then one day a dolphin strengthened my belief in the telepathy between us by immediately gifting me with a large bubble in response to my finally tuning into the message he had been trying to convey while swimming back and forth in front of me with a group of about seven other dolphins. The message was to look at his tail, which had a white scrap of material draped over it like a small scarf. When the message ultimately got through to me, and I looked at his scarf, I was instantly sent a bubble that provided me with a clear reward for finally tuning into his communication.

Following this event, I became enchanted by bubbles and constantly pleaded for more as a way to confirm that my conversations with the dolphins were real. Yet even when I succeeded in eliciting a bubble, I would ask for another. Over time, this became my favorite symbol of understanding between the dolphins and me, and each time I received the gift of a bubble, I felt more assured that the dolphins and I were conversing.

Several months after this system of reward was established, a friend invited me to join her for a week of swimming with the dolphins on the Big Island. Before going, I sent out a request for bubbles, as well as an invitation to play the leaf game, since the Big Island was where the game had originated with Joan Ocean, one of the first to connect with the spinners in their beautiful Kealakekua Bay. This was fairly early in my ten-year journey with the dolphins, and it was my first time swimming with the ones on the Big Island.

I was delighted to see these dolphins already playing in our bow waves as we were leaving the harbor early on our first morning and felt assured that we would have a good day. Before long, the dolphins reduced their swimming speed and began to slowly circle our boat, prompting our captain to also cut his speed. Next, they drew a bit closer, requiring him to go even slower. And, then they completely stopped, indicating a desire to swim with us. One of them positioned himself alongside the boat next to me with a garbage bag on his tail, which I assumed was in response to my request to play the passing game. As he watched me gather my gear, he deftly moved his bag from his tail to his dorsal fin, then to his flipper and back to his tail again, clearly inviting me to play.

I slipped into the water next to him with the intention of accepting his invitation, but I was unexpectedly distracted by a jolt of panic when I glanced down at the ocean floor through my mask and realized I couldn't see the bottom. Quite different from the sandy bottom of the beach on Oʻahu where I had done all of my swimming with dolphins up to this point, the seamless, open ocean fell hundreds of feet away from me and completely out of sight. Even though I was a lifelong swimmer and surfer, as well as a lifeguard and swim instructor, I had never been dropped into the ocean from a boat before, so I had no idea it would feel so different from swimming offshore where a sandy floor was always reassuringly in sight.

Apparently in response to the shock of fear surging involuntarily from my gut out into the ocean, five dolphins gathered about ten feet beneath me, forming a temporary floor for me to look at for comfort. When they stayed there until I settled down, I realized their help was intentional, and I have never again felt uncomfortable swimming among other species in the seemingly endless depths of the open ocean.

When these dolphins eventually moved away from my floor arrangement, one released a large bubble that floated directly up to me. When I squealed with delight, he released another, and when I squealed again, he sent me one more. It seemed that these dolphins had, in fact, heard my request for bubbles and were responding without the same reserve or teasing I had endured from the Oʻahu dolphins. Interestingly, once we were back on our boat, the guides exclaimed that they had not seen so many bubbles, nor such large ones, on prior trips.

A World Alive with Communication

Although it took me a while to trust in the telepathy of dolphins, when I finally accepted the possibility of this phenomenon, it opened up a whole new world to me, one alive with conversation! And once I tuned in, it wasn't long before I noticed that the fish I had begun to notice when I was first looking for dolphins were even more alert and responsive to my thoughts than I had previously perceived, as were the turtles and the rays. In fact, whenever I consciously sent waves of love into the ocean in an effort to attract dolphins, these other marine friends seemed to tune into the energy and would often change the course they were on and swim toward me.

I have similarly observed butterflies, birds, and even bees and others on land respond to the energies of love when sent into the world or directly to them, and I've noticed that telepathic transmissions work with domesticated animals as well. In fact, one amusing story surfaced during a dinner party with friends at their home where I was a houseguest. I had fallen in love with their wonderful German shepherd, Karma, who was sitting under the dinner table between his mistress and me as we talked well into the night. Eventually, Karma began to get restless and pawed my foot, while looking at me pleadingly as if to ask if we would ever stop talking. So, I threw some thoughts his way to keep him more included in our conversation. Knowing he wanted to get to bed, one of my thoughts was to ask, "Do you ever sleep in the bed with your mistress and master?"

When I joined the family and their other houseguests for a popover breakfast the following morning. My friend knew how much I enjoyed her dog, so couldn't wait to tell me that Karma had jumped onto their bed that night—something he had never done before. I quickly told her about the question I had sent to him during dinner, and because she already believed Karma to be telepathic, my confession solved her mystery.

Once we become aware of telepathy, we have an explanation for how dogs and cats and even pigs and other pets are able to respond appropriately to their owners' needs for help, as reported on the news. It also explains why biologist Rupert Sheldrake was able to tape images of pets jumping off sofas and running excitedly to their front doors to wait at the exact moment their owners were gathering their things at the office in order to head home.

Of additional interest, the consciousness that many of us sense animals have is supported by the animals who have been taught to speak to us in languages we can understand. For example, the famous parrot, Alex, had learned enough vocabulary to robustly express himself and was able to share more of his consciousness than we dreamed possible for a bird, even indicating when he wanted to end a training session to get a shower and his supper.

Similarly, Koko, the famed signing gorilla, was able to include herself in conversations between others, even when signing was not used, and would sometimes reveal her ability to telepathically eavesdrop by adding a comment that matched the topic. During a car ride with her trainer, Koko was also able to sense the feelings of a horse carrying a rider along the roadside and expressed her compassion for the horse due to his "mouth hurting" because of "something" in it.

With my growing awareness of a conversation in our midst, I decided to join it one day while driving home from the beach by sending love—and a request to turn around and say hi—to a horse being pulled in a small trailer traveling in my lane ahead of me. I was shocked when this horse soon took great pains to turn his head all the way around to offer me a long look.

Since that day I've communicated with many other animals and young children crossing my path and delight in how often they clearly respond with a turn of the head, a long look, or a smile. I've even sent soothing energy and comforting thoughts to babies crying on airplanes and am always both surprised and pleased when a number of them seem to settle right down.

Telepathy also explains some unusual communications taking place in the plant world that are validated by a number of studies, including many done by former CIA operative Cleve Backster, as described in his book *Primary Perception: Biocommunication with Plants, Living Foods, and Human Cells.* His early studies showed that plants with electrodes clipped to their leaves were able to register both recognition and fear of the person who had shredded the plant sitting next to them.

When I met Cleve briefly at his lab, he shared that studies conducted after the release of his book revealed even more dramatic things such as a conscious response on the part of eggs registering overexcitement on electrodes attached to their shells when neighboring eggs were being broken and cooked.

If birds and dogs and gorillas and plants—and even eggs—can tune in to the collective discussion, surely the large-brained dolphins and whales are able to communicate telepathically. There is clearly a conversation in our midst that we have not been privy to, as a result of our belief that we are the only ones able to converse. What a surprise to discover that other species are not only communicating within their own groups, but with each other as well—and that they've probably been eavesdropping on us to boot! How embarrassing to discover that we're possibly the only ones who've been excluded from this collective conversation, while everyone else is in on the secret. Ironically, our pomposity has walled us off from this rich and delightful connection, and the joke is on us.

The question is, will we be able to set aside our pride in order to tune in late, or will we persist in discounting and even ridiculing this delightful exchange going on all around us? Should we ever decide to tune in, we will discover a fascinating world currently operating outside of our awareness—such as birds with opinions, chatty gorillas, and conscious eggs. We will also become more aware of our connection to this engaging world and will inevitably care more about it and take better care of it.

The Cost of Losing Our Telepathic Skills

So how did humans—who consider themselves to be at the top of the heap—end up without the skill of telepathy, even though more than 50 percent of people secretly believe that telepathy is possible, and it's arguably the most natural, efficient, and complete form of communication?

To understand what happened, it's important to realize that most of our babies are initially adept at this invisible form of communicating with us, and many parents are at least mildly aware of a telepathic connection with their infants as they unconsciously respond to their silent calls for help. Although this responding to our pre-verbal children is primarily in the background of our awareness, anytime a message is broadcast by a child in dire need of help, the transmission will be both strong and clear, and is less likely to go unnoticed or to be filtered, doubted, or ignored.

In my case, a telepathic call of alarm from one of my children suffocating (while caught under the mattress of her collapsed crib) impelled me to abruptly hang up the phone on my sister without explanation. Then, without knowing why, I followed my intense urge to run down the hall in the nick of time to save my child who had begun to turn blue.

This urgent call for help from my child constituted my first telepathic communication that was both strongly sent and clearly received. It felt like a bundle of information sent on the wings of strong emotion, transmitted to me through several walls of our house from her bedroom, about eighty feet away, letting me know that my napping child had an emergency requiring my help. Although it was a moderately complex package of information, I received the whole message as a unit and was able to quickly discern that it was a crisis requiring my immediate response. I didn't realize until years later that I had employed the critical tool of telepathy—which would have greatly enhanced my parenting had I understood its value and continued to use it.

I had heard about indigenous parents from other cultures using telepathy to communicate with their children. But, like the majority of American parents who discount this ability, I failed to understand that my early telepathic understanding of my child was not an anomaly, but was a high-level skill I possessed and could have cultivated had I known its value or how to more mindfully access it. Yet, in the absence of understanding or using this skill in the context of my culture, it atrophied in me and ultimately in my children, resulting in our loss of the ability to communicate in this highly efficient and wholly transparent and honest manner.

Sadly, telepathy has not only fallen into the realm of being ignored in our culture, but is often scorned—if not feared—as occult in nature. As a result, we've lost our awareness of this natural, yet advanced form of communication, and our failure to keep it alive and active has caused this skill to atrophy in most of us. Unfortunately, the exclusively verbal communication we are then forced to use not only cuts us off from the richer and deeper conversations that telepathy supports, but also results in a serious separation of our hearts from nature and others with whom we share this world.

Our solely verbal, non-telepathic communication has also enabled more and more dishonorable and dishonest people to get away with telling lies and hiding their transgressions from increasingly large segments of the population, often without consequence. It's this growing virus of deception that lies at the core of our crisis of personal and moral decline and the growing destruction of each other and other species—and our planetary home.

Yet, even in the midst of the unkindness and chaos this virus is able to create in the absence of telepathy, many of us know when others are not doing the right thing and can sense who the troublemakers are. This is because we are not fully cut off from our telepathic skills and could reclaim them if we grasped the importance of doing so—just as I was able to reclaim some of mine during my time with the dolphins.

Exposing All Things Hidden

Once I realized how easily telepathy exposes ignoble thoughts and hidden agendas, I could see that living in a telepathic world would inspire better behavior in my own society, starting with myself. This motivated me to begin the process of not simply trying to hide my tarnished thoughts, but of cleaning them up so that they were the kinds of thoughts I could happily expose. And by setting this goal, I focused on things that helped me to become a better person.

I first noticed my need to improve my thoughts on a day when I had been swimming with the dolphins for several hours and was getting cold and a little bored, but didn't feel free to get out of the water until the dolphins had left. The moment I had this thought, the happy chirping and chatter of the dolphins stopped so abruptly and simultaneously that it seemed as if a symphony conductor had brought his forefinger and thumb together to end a score. The dolphins then quietly left the area and didn't return for the remainder of the day. I realized instantly that they had telepathically overheard my ability to get bored in the midst of their giving me the gift of never-ending joy, and I felt deeply embarrassed.

On another occasion, my critical thoughts about a peculiar looking dolphin in Australia of a different species than I was used to seeing prompted him to dive to escape my judgment. While still in Australia, after being highly entertained by two remarkable whales riding our bow wave for over an hour, a lone dolphin took their place at our bow right after the whales had left. When I carelessly viewed this dolphin as small and insignificant in contrast to the larger-than-life whales, he sent me a wave of energy carrying his hurt as he dove to leave. I was horrified.

It became painfully clear to me following these two events that our thoughts and judgments are carried telepathically out into the world, where they impact and hurt others, even when we think they're private and unheard. I was not only mortified by being overheard, but carried the hurt of those dolphins in my heart for quite some time.

Conversations Throughout the Sea

By the time it sank into my awareness that a conversation exists among cetaceans, as well as between them and other species, life around me became more animated, alive, and fun. I was also now able to understand the claim I had heard others make that once you've swum with dolphins and whales, other dolphins and whales from around the world will recognize you, likely due to transparent conversations between them. Even before hearing about this, I had noticed that wherever I traveled, the dolphins and whales in each new area seemed to greet me with recognition.

They also consistently presented me with bubbles, as if they knew they were the calling cards I would recognize and enjoy. In fact, over time, it appeared that the primary way dolphins across the globe used to convince me that I understood their thoughts was to send me bubbles—big bubbles, small bubbles, ringed bubbles, and cloud bubbles. But I was insatiable, so I would ask for more bubbles to assure myself that they could understand me. Not only did the bubbles help to convince me I was not imagining things, they also anchored me in something tangible and real in the midst of my otherwise surreal experience of communicating with another species.

Yet even though the dolphins responded to my requests for more bubbles, they did so in their own playful and unpredictable manner. Thus, although the cherished bubbles came in many sizes and shapes, and from dolphins all over the world, they always came on the dolphins' terms, rather than mine. This unpredictable delivery of the bubbles added to their magic and my delight, and I came to view them as wonderfully precious gifts. Yet no matter how many bubbles the dolphins sent, I persisted in holding onto small doubts about their role in confirming a telepathic communication between us.

Then one day, complete satisfaction came. I had felt compelled to visit our local marine park in order to connect, as I had promised, with the dolphins that had been moved there from the hotel's dolphin lagoon a few months earlier. When I arrived at the park's central dolphin tank, a female named Laka swam over to greet me. As I asked Laka's trainer about where I might find the hotel dolphins who had been moved to their facility, Laka engaged me in a prolonged gaze. I was enjoying this encounter and felt rather special and chosen when the trainer informed me that Laka was the dominant dolphin in this tank. In fact, as Laka continued her unbroken gaze, the trainer explained how the staff had recently deduced that when the other dolphins weren't cooperating, it was likely because Laka had told them not to comply. Sadly, the trainers were now using their discovery to separate Laka from the other dolphins.

But rather than sulk, this strong dolphin used my visit as an opportunity to hold onto some form of control and pleasure in life. In fact, while I was absorbing the news that the trainers had separated her from the others, I noticed a slight ripple run through Laka's body as a naughty twinkle lit up her eye. Just as I was trying to understand what was happening, she splashed me with a sizable wall of water. I was shocked and looked down at my drenched clothes to find that she had truly nailed me. I quickly looked up at Laka in time to see her entire face light up, her eyes flashing gleefully back into mine. I couldn't help bursting out laughing. Laka then surprised me again by mimicking my boisterous laugh perfectly, which made me laugh even harder. Next, Laukani from a nearby tank joined in the fun with her loud version of my laugh, and I laughed even harder still, as did both dolphins, until the three of us got downright hysterical.

After I recovered from this very dolphin-like encounter, the baffled trainer took me downstairs to watch the dolphins from their underwater observation station. The moment we got to the curved surveillance window, Laka was there, waiting for us. I put my hand on the window, and Laka nuzzled her cheek into my hand from the other side as I sent love from my hand to her through the glass. She remained there, gazing steadily at me as the trainer and I talked.

While continuing to hold Laka's unblinking gaze, I asked the trainer if the captive dolphins blew bubbles in their pool like the dolphins in the open ocean do. The moment my question was framed, Laka released an enormous bubble that caught both of our attention to the point of pausing our conversation. But then the trainer, who had previously informed me that she didn't believe in dolphin telepathy, recomposed herself and continued with her description of the park's program without any mention of the bubble.

I was thrilled by Laka's public demonstration of understanding between us, and I hoped to draw more of the trainer's attention to what had just happened. So I looked at Laka and said aloud, "You heard me ask about the bubbles, didn't you?" Maintaining our steady gaze, Laka answered with a twinkle that again danced in her eye.

Realizing the observation area was probably being videotaped to collect information for research, I asked aloud for more bubbles. Laka hesitated for a few moments but then, with another mischievous glint in her eye produced a stream of the tiniest bubbles I had ever seen. I laughed again at how this alpha female had found a way to respond to my request, while remaining in control under circumstances that afforded her very little opportunity to take the lead. Laka then offered me one final dance in her eyes, as I squealed and thanked her for the tiny bubbles.

Later, as I prepared to leave this area to continue my search for my hotel dolphin friends, I turned to say goodbye to Laka. As our eyes locked, I silently asked for one more bubble, which she immediately released along with a soulful, less mischievous gaze. Tears spilled down my cheeks as I walked away, my heart filled with emotion. Not only had I enjoyed this delightful encounter with the funny and dominant Laka, I had also—finally—accepted once and for all that the dolphins understand and communicate with me. I further deduced that dolphins are telepathic communicators with each other as well—and with anyone who is tuned in and listening.

Even more poignant was the fact that this proud alpha dolphin had surrendered to my requests for bubbles in the presence of a third party in control of her life. Although the trainer shared that she had been advised not to look for telepathic communication or to attach too much importance to it, she had noticed. Even more important, I was finally convinced that the dolphins and I were in fact holding a conversation. It had taken me ten years and many bubbles to surrender to this truth. And I was grateful to Laka for finally getting through to me.

As I left the viewing area, I silently promised Laka that I would put aside my embarrassment about believing in telepathy or using it to converse with dolphins. I would also come out of my closet of fear to broadcast the secrets they had shared about ways humanity can also live with the wisdom, love, harmony, and joy found only through the clarity and truth that results from a telepathically seamless and honest world.

Finally accepting that I was at the heart of an interspecies communication through the common language of telepathy allowed me to see that telepathy had opened up my own world in new and powerful ways. I could also see that if humanity would surrender to trusting and using this skill, that we too could live with the same openness, honesty, and clarity on land as the dolphins enjoy beneath the sea.

I decided to hold myself to this standard and made a commitment to live my life as if I reside in a telepathic world in which everyone can read my thoughts. To fulfill my goal of complete openness and honesty in a world not yet telepathic, I have learned to expose my thoughts and actions voluntarily, first to myself and then to others. This has motivated me to keep my thoughts clean and kind, and the better I get at this level of transparency, the clearer, more mature, and kinder I have become.

But, I didn't fully understand why this level of honesty had proved to be so powerful until I ran across the claim of the late psychiatrist, Dr. David Viscott, who once brilliantly noted that our mental illness and mental health lie along the same continuum as our honesty and secrets. Accordingly, the greater our truth, the greater our emotional health will be, while the more we allow deception to creep into ourselves and our culture, the more our mental illness will manifest.

Clearly, truth has been slipping away in our society, and our mental health has been declining with it. But, we can bring it back if we embrace the power of telepathy and use it, not only to fully hear and care about the needs of others, but to also face and stop putting up with the rampant deception in our midst. Committing to this level of transparency and honesty would be of value to our entire society in the same way it benefits the dolphins to live in the clarity of their telepathic and transparent world.

Clarity is achieved through complete and honest communications that pull us all the way out of the shadows and into the light.

CHAPTER 8

Trait #6: The Power of the Heart

Spin and weave a wondrous dance of Love.

The more I was able to communicate with the dolphins, the better I could see that the real magic between us lay not in the method they used to converse with me, but in what they were saying. I also noticed that the longer I listened, the more evident it became that the dolphins weren't showing me their six Higher Self traits just to impress me. They were showing me how I could also become my best Self and to inspire my species to do the same.

The Gift of the Dolphins' Larger Message

After several years under the dolphins' tutelage, I began to wonder why they were investing so much of their time to help me understand how life works behind the scenes at the invisible, quantum level and to inspire me to use this information to become a more loving person and my own Higher Self.

In my effort to answer my question about why they were doing this, I realized their lessons were a gift of love they would give to anyone—to you, to me, to anyone—who is willing to listen and learn. And the more interest I showed in what they were sharing, the more they revealed and the more I learned.

This was just one of the many ways the dolphins express their sixth and most important Higher Self trait of loving kindness—by offering generous amounts of their time to humans and others, no matter what level of our own kindness we have achieved.

The Loving Nature of Dolphins

Although I was already in awe of the unfolding mosaic of the dolphins' Higher Self traits, their loving nature is the trait that impresses me the most. This particular quality—also woven through each of the dolphins' other Higher Self traits—is exemplified by their ability to remain so steadily in a loving state under all circumstances. And, because this ability raises their loving vibrations to such palpably magical and joyful levels, we can also vicariously experience the joy and magic when in their presence.

This is the baseline from which dolphins operate. And it's the strength of this soft force of love—similar to the peaceful power of enlightened masters—that draws us irresistibly toward them.

The Magic of Love

So, what is it about being imbued with loving kindness that makes those able to achieve it so admired and adored by others? And, what is it about the trait of love that makes it the most important of all the dolphins' traits and the one that seems to both empower and sweeten their lives and ours whenever we're lucky enough to be in their presence?

Why do our hearts automatically light up when we see a dolphin leap into the air, approach our boats, or glide beneath us as we swim in the ocean? Why does such a strong spark of love ignite in our hearts the moment we see one or more of these unique and playful beings, seemingly drenched in love? And, why does that spark magnify and vibrate evermore intensely and at higher frequencies, the closer we get to them and the longer we stay?

By igniting our hearts with the love held in theirs, are the dolphins showing us just how blissful our world could be if we embodied the essence of love as strongly as they do? Most of us have had periodic glimpses of what it's like to feel so flooded with the energy of love that all seems right with the world. And if we pay even closer attention, we will also notice that it's during those times when our relationships and lives go unusually well and our dreams—apparently attracted to the energy—seem to pop up out of nowhere to draw near and slip into our lives.

I had not made this connection between the times when my heart was filled with love and the increase in my own good fortune until one day I noticed that the dolphins seem to be continually immersed in a loving state as they travel the oceans with glee. It was in the midst of observing this connection between their loving natures and their continuous state of joy that I noticed the same is also true for me. I realized that the times when I'm engaged in loving kindness toward others are also the times when my life works at its best. So, why does this happen? And, what's behind this connection between our most loving selves and our good fortune?

The Reason Good Hearts Attract Good Luck

Science demonstrates that we all vibrate energetically at various frequencies, based solely on what we are thinking, feeling, and doing. Thus, the more we think and act in kind and loving ways, the more we raise the frequency of our vibrations. And, the higher our frequencies, the more we attract positive events, people, and emotions to ourselves, and to our children, based on the principle that like attracts like.

The obverse is also true: whenever we focus on our grievances about the past or our fears about the future, these depleting concerns lower our vibrations, which, in turn, attract low vibration experiences to us. This is again simply because like attracts like.

Due to the way this works, our good fortune is in direct proportion to the amount of kind compassion and love we invite to flow through our hearts, which explains why love serves as the magnet, and thus the source of all good things being attracted to us and to humanity as a whole. It also explains why abiding love is the most potent of the dolphins' Higher Self traits and is the one that elevates their notably high vibrations and the resulting magic those vibrations draw to them and to our world.

How Loving Vibrations Pull Good Fortune to Us

The dolphins' bubble diagrams (discussed in chapter 6) provide us with animated drawings of the otherwise invisible workings of how our world works, including the details of how love draws more love and goodness to our lives and how hate invokes the opposite result.

We can see from these diagrams that whenever our hearts are filled with hate, our hateful energies are sent "spinning" out into the world and universe, where they impact others with the energy of our hate. They then come back to us on the return spin of the toroidal arc, now filled with our original hate, plus the impact our hate has had on others.

But, if we're filled with loving vibrations, those vibrations are also continuously sent spinning out from us into the world and beyond, where they bring back more loving energy on the return spin, now filled with our original loving vibrations, plus the impact they have had on others.

Interestingly, the dolphins' diagrams showing us how to keep love circulating and growing matches the Stanford University-based HeartMath Institute's discoveries. But the Institute goes further. It suggests that the spiraling force of all life is not only powered by the energy of love, but will constrict and slow down—and eventually stop and die—if compassion and caring fail to flow through the energetic pathways of the forces of life.

In alignment with the Institute's theory, it seems the dolphins' bubble drawings are not just showing us how to keep love flowing for the sake of all of our survival, but are also revealing how the love we send to others finds its way back to us to then saturate our own lives. Thus, if the Institute and dolphins understand this correctly, love not only enables us to survive, but is also the force that blesses our lives.

Are the dolphins' diagrams also showing us that manifesting the lives and world we want is more achievable than we've thought—simply by using our power of choice to commit to being loving in all that we do?

And, is their own deep reservoir of love the thing that powers the dolphins leaps from just below the water's surface to twirl multiple times through the air, as they visibly throw their healing, love, and joy into the world? And, is it this same power of love that gracefully twirls whales into soft pirouettes beneath the sea and then powerfully thrusts their massive tonnage spiraling into the air?

Finally, and of even more interest and importance—are the dolphins agreeing with the HeartMath Institute's hypothesis: that love is not only the force that fuels all aspects of life—from the tiniest spinning photon to the dramatic spiraling of the galaxies—but that it's the only force? If so, do the dolphins also agree with the Institute's prediction that if we fail to keep this essential force of love flowing, we simply won't survive?

If this plausible hypothesis is true, we have a clear choice to make between continuing on our current course of unkindness or becoming a reliably loving species. But since we've failed to adopt the loving option to date, what will prompt us to choose it now? I offer an answer to this question in Chapter 16 ("Real Hope for Humanity"), based on a new discovery in science, coupled with my observations of how the dolphins and whales do it.

The Power of Choosing to Be Loving

Had I grasped at any point along the course of my life the profound damage to my own good fortune that angry regrets and unloving thoughts toward others can cause, I would have lost all interest in engaging in this popular, but careless and even dangerous, cultural pastime.

Or, if I had known the boundless amount of love and great fortune I could have drawn to myself and then placed in the vortex of my heart to send out to others and back to me, multiplied, in our ever-spiraling universal flow of energy, I would have chosen love as steadfastly as the dolphins do.

Once the dolphins were able to make this insight clear for me about the state of my heart creating either a reservoir of loving or unloving energy that will, in turn, pull its likeness to me, I made the most important decision of my life. I made a decision that would help me to fill my heart's reservoir with loving energy, as I witnessed the dolphins doing, and to then send that ample collection of love out to others on the ever-spinning exchange of energy between all of our hearts in the web of this entangled Universe.

The Decision

As I was absorbing the full impact of the importance of the energy we send into the world—both because it matters for others and because it comes back to us—I made a decision to more steadily collect and hold love in my heart.

To help me feel centered enough to honor this commitment, I returned to starting my days with journaling, meditation, and walking. The combination of this routine plus swimming with dolphins made it easier for me to hang out in my heart and send loving energy into the world and to others.

The Seat of My Higher Self

I also noticed around this time that whenever I entered my counseling room and sat in my therapy chair, I would rather quickly slide into my heart and Higher Self that I had been working on strengthening. Both my clients and I benefitted from this more centered and caring persona, and spending so much of my time in the chair of my Higher Self was reinforcing my ability to hold love in my heart. I could sense that this better self was not only attractive to clients and others, but also seemed to attract more unexpected good fortune to me, in addition to the specific dreams I was calling to my life.

Then one day, it clicked. Why wouldn't I take that same Higher Self with me as I walked out the door of my counseling room to my car and then continue to hold onto it while driving home, greeting my children, and spending the evening with my family? I couldn't come up with a reason why I wouldn't give my own family the benefit of the best self I had been sharing with my clients during the day.

So I made a vow to take my Higher Self home with me and to keep it there, not just for the evening, but during all of my time with my family. I later expanded this vow to taking it with me wherever I go. And, although I still periodically slip out of my Higher Self, the vow has helped me to more steadily hold onto that better place within myself. This has clearly served me, and those who cross my path, well. And it has helped me to build an even larger reservoir of love to serve as a magnet to the goodness of life.

Embodying and Teaching the Mastery of Love

Once I understood that the dolphins—and later the whales— were acting as my instructors, I could see how uniquely qualified they are to teach our species how to live as our Higher Selves and to achieve the same kind of mastery and grace on land that they have achieved in the sea. Not only are they worthy models of how to be our Higher Selves, they have successfully manifested a culture filled with wisdom, love, harmony, and joy, which magnetically draws humans like me—and others—to want to spend time with them in their love-drenched world.

By modeling the traits of the Higher Self for us, while also teaching us how to manifest our own miracles, the dolphins offer humanity a simple formula for being our best and most loving selves, poised to create the world of our dreams. We need only to recognize these lessons and apply them if we wish to achieve the same state of harmony on our shores as the dolphins and whales have achieved in the sea.

To begin, we can weave the six traits of the Higher Self that the cetaceans embody—including the final and most important one of loving kindness—into our own molecular structure and DNA. Not only will this enable us to live in our greatness and bring heaven to earth, it will enable us to dance more freely with the same mastery and grace the dolphins display, as they leap and twirl their way across our horizons.

Dance your way to heaven on earth.

PART III

Creating the World of Your Dreams: Six Insights for Manifesting Your Goals

O ver time, I noticed that the dolphins' lessons for helping our species to live with as much magic and joy as they do are divided into two parts. The first part shows us how to be our best selves. The second part provides new ways we can manifest our dreams. Together, these lessons of character and power create a tapestry for how to live our best lives as our best selves.

Thus, in addition to teaching us how to be our best selves through the process of adopting the six traits of the Higher Self shared in Part II, the dolphins also provided me with six insights on how to powerfully manifest the lives we most want to live, which I share in this section, Part III.

They did this by showing me a new way that we humans can act as our Higher Selves, while at the same time rather easily manifesting our dreams. When used together, the combination proves to be even more powerful and life-changing.

Although some of the dolphins' manifesting insights overlap with other manifesting programs, the dolphins have added a few critical keys that are missing from the other formulas, while also excluding some of their ideas that seem to actually impede success. Thus, even though I had used a number of the other approaches with a fair measure of success, the dolphins' unique manifesting tips enabled me to enjoy my most miraculous results, while also being the easiest to learn and the most fun to follow.

A Tapestry of Traits and Insights

As I wove the strands of the dolphins' manifesting insights together with the Higher Self traits they embody, a stunning tapestry emerged that revealed the source of the dolphins' renowned magic and humanity's greatest possibilities. Yet even though the dolphins' traits and insights are integrally woven together, for the sake of clarity I have separated their Higher Self qualities previously listed in Part II from their manifesting insights that I now present here in Part III as follows.

CHAPTER 9

Manifesting Insight #1: Clearly Select and Strongly Yearn for Your Dreams Until They Arrive

Send out thoughts filled with your dreams and emotions filled with your desires to prepare the path for the future you want.

In order to understand why I was able as a child to enlist the strength of my yearning to succeed in pulling my dream of going horseback riding to me and later as an adult of swimming with dolphins, it helps to understand the science behind how this works.

Quantum physics explains that sending the emotion of our desires into the Universal "Field" for planting results in those desires being drawn back to us. This helps to explain why we are able to pull from the Universal Field whatever we're most vigorously focused on (including both our strong desires and strong fears). But, biology makes it even easier to visualize and understand how this works.

Here's why. Biologist Candace Pert discovered that anytime we fill our hearts with an intense yearning for something such as love, our personal chemistry responds to our yearning by forming *ligands* that alter their shape into the form of a hook designed to both search for and hook onto the matching shape of love. They do this by wiggling and shimmying and even humming in order to vibrationally align their shape to match the shape of the receptor molecules of what they seek (in this case love), which is also aligning itself to become a receptor match to the ligands in search of it. Likewise, whenever we're filled with the strong energy of anger toward others, our chemistry is altered to form ligands shaped to both find and hook anger receptors to us.

We can extrapolate from this model that if you want love in your life, it's essential to fill your heart with both the essence and the desire for love, and if you want to swim with dolphins, it's important to fill your heart with yearning for the essence of that experience. It also explains why sending strong waves of energy filled with our various desires, prayers, and intentions out into the world has such a powerful influence on the world, seemingly eager and waiting to match its receptors to the energies and hooks we send out in search of them.

Once I grasped the picture of how this works, I realized that the first of the manifesting insights I had learned from the dolphins lies in the importance of more clearly identifying and selecting our dreams as well as more actively yearning for them until they arrive.

When I first thought about swimming with dolphins, my interest in this activity was not clear. Neither was it strong. In fact, it began as an item on a long list of things I wistfully hoped to do someday, simply because I had seen it on someone else's list. I had no real image of what this might look like or when it would take place. As a result of my soft interest in this hazy dream with a fuzzy timeline, swimming with dolphins evolved in perfect proportion to the place it held on my list and in my heart. In fact, connecting with dolphins didn't come into full focus or find its way to me until several years later when my interest in actually having this experience began to gel.

Yet even as my interest in swimming with dolphins increased over time, my desire was still not as strong as needed to bring it to full fruition. The dolphins made me aware of how wobbly my desire to swim with them was when they showed up at Makua Beach full of vim and vigor and ready to rock and roll at a time when I was there with a friend. We were checking out the conditions in preparation for our plan to swim with the dolphins the following day with the rest of our group who had gathered at a nearby hotel to celebrate my upcoming fiftieth birthday.

But, the dolphins' arrival a day early was not in sync with the plan I had devised, and the rest of our group was at the hotel warming up for a tennis round robin, scheduled to start in an hour. So, rather than jump into the water to play with the frisky and welcoming dolphins, my friend and I returned to the hotel to join the others for tennis. In making this choice, I naively assumed the dolphins would return the next day, in accordance with my schedule and when our full party would be there to enjoy them. But, the dolphins were on their own schedule, not mine. So, the following morning, when our group arrived at the beach eager to swim with the dolphins as planned, we could hear them chirping and spent an hour chasing after their sounds. But when the dolphins made a point of not showing us their faces or getting close enough to play, it dawned on me that I had missed my chance to swim with them the previous day when I had chosen to play tennis instead.

Paradoxically, my desire to play tennis had not been strong enough for me to engage in the game enthusiastically or to play well, and it occurred to me in the middle of the match that I had not succeeded in either playing good tennis or swimming with the dolphins.

The dolphins' avoidance of our group the next day offered further evidence that my splintered choice between them and tennis wasn't effective, and that I would be wise to sharpen the clarity of my goals in conjunction with strengthening my desire to fulfill them.

Actively Yearn for Your Dreams

Following my birthday weekend, I felt disappointed that I had missed my chance to swim with the dolphins, and my lingering regret over having ignored their welcoming window for playing together ignited an even stronger desire in me to make this connection.

My newly elevated desire to connect with wild dolphins reminded me of how I had felt as a child, when strong feelings of desire about doing things had come so naturally. I particularly remembered an incident that occurred during a summer I was spending with my friend on the Big Island of Hawai'i. She and I were fervently hoping the rain would stop so the skies could clear enough for us to go horseback riding at Kahua Ranch in Waimea. My friend and I kept looking at the sky in search of a blue patch big enough to qualify as a pair of Dutchman's pants in order to meet the criterion her mother had set for us to proceed with our plan. Our mutual, intense yearning to see a blue patch in the sky seemed to produce a small one. But, when her mother said it had to be a larger patch of blue, big enough to fit an adult Dutchman, we again yearned together as we watched the blue pants in the sky slowly grow. Our intense desire to go horseback riding was fulfilled, and I continued after that day to strongly yearn for many other experiences throughout my childhood, experiences that also materialized. Yet, I had no idea at the time that I was engaged in conscious manifesting, with my yearning serving as the engine of my success. And due to my failure to understand the connection between my yearning and my good results, over time, the yearning dropped away.

Upon remembering this story, I decided to revive the feelings of excitement and passion I had so naturally felt as a child wanting to go horseback riding. And so, I consciously summoned similar feelings of yearning to swim with the dolphins and fanned those feelings in my heart. In time, the intensity of my increased desire stirring in my heart began to serve as a conduit for connecting me to the dolphins, and before long they responded to the call and showed up to swim with me.

Stay with Your Dreams Until They're Fulfilled

Staying with the dreams you've selected until they're fulfilled is the second—yet vitally important—aspect of the dolphins' first insight for manifesting. Not only does "sticking with it" distinguish the dolphins' manifesting program from others, it's also the feature that makes their program so uniquely successful.

This "sticking with it" component recommends not viewing your dream requests as a one-off appeal to then be released to the Universe to fulfill for you. The reason for this caution is that relaxing the passion of your desire for your dreams to find you will cause the intensity of your yearning to peter out, similar to an unmailed love letter left on the desk or sitting in your outbox.

Thus, at any time or at any point your yearning for a dream weakens along the way—whether at the beginning, the middle, or the end—your dream will likely let go of you as well and drift off to go elsewhere. So, instead of "letting go" or "releasing your dreams to the Universe," actively holding your desire for the dreams you select to vibrate in your heart will help you to stay connected to those dreams until they respond and show up in your life.

This is done via the process of steadily yearning and thus vibrating and jiggling the universal strings connecting you to your dreams within the web of our nonlocal and entangled Universe, in which everything—both near and far—is linked to everything else. By keeping your connection to your dreams active via the humming and purring and jiggling of vibrations linking you, you give them the time they need to get aligned with your likeness as they pull toward you until you are eventually hooked.

Interestingly, a person who is intensely yearned for can often telepathically sense the vibrational attention of the yearner focused on them and may begin to yearn for the yearner in return, causing the two to be drawn even more magnetically toward one another. In my case, the dolphins not only responded to my vibrational yearning and calling for them, but in time they also called me to them. I realized from the viewpoint of the one being called how powerful the urge to respond can be, particularly when the yearner's call is sent with the added force of intense emotion, especially the emotion of love. It's as if, "What you yearn for, also yearns for you," and I was pleased to be more consciously engaged in this delightfully magnetic dance—between the wanter and the wanted, the lover and the beloved, and the desirer and the desired—that lies at the core of all of our manifestations. Yet, the success of this dance only works if you are a vibrational match to your dream. So, if you hope to attract dolphins, it's important that you raise your vibrations to match theirs. And if you hope to raise the level of your good fortune, the same is also true.

Being on the receiving end of the dolphins' yearning made me more aware that if I call people and events to me in a similarly sustained manner, they will be more likely to notice the jiggling of my yearning vibrations and, in turn, feel pulled to respond. This call-and-response process is not only a critical component of the magic of creation, but is perfectly designed to work.

Being Crystal Clear and Laser Focused

Now that we understand how and why our intense focus on something will likely pull it to us, we can also see why it's so important not to carelessly focus on our doubts or fears, since doing so will invariably add them to our list of requests—and our results.

Yet, this is often easier said than done, since anytime we unleash our desire for something we ardently want, we often also unleash our fear that we might not get it. Fortunately, learning to contain and tame these fears with techniques such as meditation and EFT Tapping (as described in Note #1) can be of help. The process of acknowledging and facing our fears, while not elevating their status to the point of inviting them to move into our minds and take over our lives can be a delicate dance. Thus, although it's critical to acknowledge our fears and to know what they are, it's also important to break the habit of greeting them like royalty whenever they show up or to metaphorically invite them in for a latte or tea and a long cozy chat between old friends.

It's equally important to pay close attention to all of our random and recurring thoughts, since it's not just our carefully selected goals that are in line to come true; our unconsciously sloppy, yet habitual worries will also materialize and become part of our lives. In fact, many great teachers have cautioned that because our repetitive thoughts—especially when paired with strong emotion—are likely to manifest, the things we focus on most—whether with trepidation or anticipation—are the things that will herald our futures and define our destinies. And, science agrees.

Yet, in spite of my knowledge of how this works, I failed to grasp the full extent of the power of my thoughts and was thus not as careful as good sense would suggest about what I invited into my head and heart. Instead, I took periodic breaks from my positive focus in order to indulge in my regrets about the past or fears of the future, without adequate regard for the steep price I would pay for this indulgence.

In time, I also noticed that whenever I slipped into carelessly unkind thoughts about others, my good luck would diminish in proportion to this slip, and whenever I returned to more consciously kind musings, my good fortune would return. The dolphins helped me to make the connection between my thoughts and my good or bad fortune by consistently showing me their lack of attraction to me during those times when I was tarnished by unkind thoughts. Our awareness of how this process works helps us to understand that the quality of our lives is in direct proportion to the quality of our focus and thoughts.

It also explains how grace is set in motion, for anytime we elect to focus kindly and embody the energies of love, we draw the matching energies of goodwill and kindness from the Universe to ourselves, along with the good fortune goodwill draws to us.

Yearn only for good for yourself and others.

CHAPTER 10

Manifesting Insight #2: Focus Utterly and Only on the Destiny You Desire

Concentrate solely and steadily on what you want.

hen I first heard Dr. Wayne Dyer speak at a small rural church in Hawai'i, he claimed to have used his mind to pull clouds from the sky. Upon hearing such a bold proclamation from this rising author, I judged him to be a bit grandiose, causing me to veer my attention away from the remainder of his talk and use the time to write a note to a friend. It wasn't until people rose to their feet to give Dr. Dyer a standing ovation that I regretted my decision to tune out and miss his message on the power of intention to manifest our dreams.

Even though I had read the same quantum physics material that Wayne Dyer had read about the untapped power of our minds, I had never thought in terms of average people like myself, or even Wayne Dyer, actually using this power to shape our own realities. Yet, I had to ask myself why Wayne Dyer had the courage to use it, while I excluded myself from its benefits. When I couldn't answer my own question, I decided to practice manifesting a cloud, as Wayne Dyer had done, and surprised myself by pulling a small, white wisp out of a clear blue sky.

Pulling Our Dreams to Us

After succeeding with the cloud experiment, I decided to use my new power to plant a more useful picture in the universal field of potential and then practice pulling it back to me. I started by planting a picture of doubles from the dice while playing backgammon with my son, and then pulling the image of doubles to me as I rolled the dice. I entertained—and surprised—both my son and myself by how often doubles would appear whenever my focus was clear and my faith steady.

Then one day, while swimming at Makua Beach at a time when the dolphins weren't there, I decided to see if I could pull them to me out of the sea in the same way I had pulled the wisps of cloud from the sky and doubles from the dice. The first time I tried this, I planted a clear picture of the dolphins emerging out of the distant underwater haze of the vast blue ocean swimming toward me. I then began to pull them to me with strong feelings of yearning stirring in my heart. Due to my success with the cloud and dice, my focus was steady and filled with faith that they would show up. And so they did, within about five minutes. Even though I understood the theory behind how this was possible, their arrival was nonetheless startling to me, and I was left with a mixture of euphoria and disbelief in my new reality.

A week later when the dolphins weren't at the beach, I had the opportunity to see if I could pull them to me again. And, to my surprise, they showed up—although this time, they took a bit longer, perhaps because I had some feelings of fear about whether or not I could repeat this feat (or because they simply had other business to address). But even with two successes under my belt, on the morning of my third try, it took a while before I finally heard a few chirps from about a mile away. I got excited when it seemed that my theory was correct, after all, and chirped back to the distant dolphins, who chirped back at me again.

But then the dolphins stopped chirping and fell silent, and I began to doubt my ability to repeat the experiment. In the midst of my doubts, I even questioned whether or not their arrival on my first two tries had been anything more than chance. Once these fears clicked into place, I fell prey to other doubts about things not working out in my life the way I wanted. These fears had become a small, but familiar, part of my life following a significant trauma I had experienced in my mid-twenties, which was followed by some aftershocks and repeats of this trauma in my thirties and again in my forties. As with most people who've experienced trauma, these traumas had introduced the idea that really bad things can happen to me, which interfered with my ability to as confidently and consistently pull good things to me, as I had done prior to my traumas.

As I floated in the water reviewing when and how I had developed this fear of my ability to fulfill dreams, I heard another chirp, still from about a mile away, accompanied by a very strong message that the dolphins were on their way. However, the message also impressed on me that if I continued to flood my heart and head with worry and doubt, the dolphins would no longer feel drawn to my energy, which was beginning to get tainted with the scent of the fear I was entertaining. Instead, they would feel compelled to turn away from such mixed and muddied energy and go elsewhere.

This was an enormous insight for me, since it awakened me to the reality that following my traumas, I had slipped into the habit of indulging in worry and doubt about my ability to attract as much good luck to my life as I had enjoyed prior to the traumas. Thus, although I still drew many good things to my life, it was on those occasions when I particularly wanted something to happen that the fears and doubts I had absorbed during my traumas would get activated enough to fill me with doubt. And even though I had grown used to this trauma-driven program running in the background of my life, I was now learning that trauma-triggered worries were not just pulling my attention away from my goals, but were also repelling enough to stop my dreams from being drawn to me.

This information reminded me of the value of holding my focus solely on the things I desire, rather than allowing the worries and doubts that had been planted in my neural pathways during the period of my traumas to infect my energy field with fear and doubt. This insight helped me to realize that other equally unattractive emotions (such as envy, irritability, impatience, and anger) also detract from our alluring natures and thus strongly repel, rather than attract, our dreams to us.

Anytime the magnetism between us and our dreams is broken for any reason—whether it's a change in our energy or a break in our yearning for them—even dreams that were on their way drift off course and never arrive, just as the dolphins were about to do with me. This happens even when a dream we can't see is on its way as the dolphins had been with me.

The most powerful part of the dolphins' design for teaching me how to remain patient and hopeful while calling my dreams to me was chiseled into the image of the distance of about a mile between the dolphins and me. The impact of this visual occurred when the dolphins chirped from so far away, making it clear that while they were still a good distance from me, they were nevertheless on their way.

Their audible chirp distinctly defined the gap between us, which I could clearly see in my mind's eye. It was a gap I strongly wanted to close, so felt inspired by the image of the gap slowly closing to more vigorously pull the dolphins closer to me with the strength of my yearning.

This initially worked well, and I felt confident that these dolphins were on their way. But then, when their chirping stopped a second time, I no longer felt sure that they were coming. And for no clear reason, I also stopped chirping. This caused a break in the connection between us—and all chirping stopped.

The silence offered me a clear illustration of how all dreams work: they invisibly and silently draw to us in a manner that takes varying amounts of time unknown to us. And, just because we can't see or hear them, it doesn't mean they're not on their way. Nor does it mean we should give up and let go of our yearning for them—especially since it's our yearning that creates a tethering between us that pulls them toward us until they eventually arrive.

The dolphins' demonstration of how yearning works to harness our dreams and pull them to us made it clear why I needed to stop giving up so easily on dreams that had not yet arrived. I also needed to stop the habit of replacing my yearning with discouragement or worry whenever there's a delay in a dream's delivery.

As I absorbed this lesson, I wondered how often good things had been on their way to me, but due to a delay in their arrival, I had begun to worry and in the process had relinquished my focus on calling them to me. This interruption in calling my dreams to me invariably broke the magnetic bond between us, resulting in some of my dreams scattering and going in other directions.

Not wanting to lose these dolphins in the same way I had lost other things, I soothed my fears and resumed my focus, while calling the dolphins to me with the more alluring energies of desire mixed with faith in our connection and the belief that they would come. I then visualized the dolphins turning back toward me to swim in my direction, while continuing to call them from my heart. I could soon feel the vibrational yearning in my chest first hook itself to the dolphins and then magnetically pull them to me, until at last I could see the forms of their bodies emerging out of the depths of the water slowly swimming toward me as if by magic.

To my surprise, rather than respond to my squeals of delight upon seeing them, they continued to approach me in silence as if to underscore that dreams don't always announce when they're on their way or nearby. Only after the dolphins had fully arrived did they break their silence and begin to chirp and chatter exuberantly, as if to applaud me for holding onto my belief in dreams coming true.

Following our swim together that day, I emerged from the water dizzy from the experience and sat on the beach awed by the reality of my ability to manifest something so big. As I reviewed what had happened, I realized the dolphins had shown me their second insight for living life effectively. They had shown me the importance of focusing solely and steadily on my dreams without being distracted by the whisperings of fear or the repelling energies of worry and doubt. In short, they had shown me how to cut through the noises of doubt to manifest my dreams.

The Courage to Claim My Belief in Manifesting

Even though I had growing proof to support my belief in the power of using our intention to call things to us, I was hesitant to publically claim my belief in something so new to our culture. I was ironically also suspicious of others claiming they could call the dolphins to them, even after witnessing them do it and doing it myself. Strangely, I even continued to view my own success in doing this on three occasions as "unbelievable." And, I certainly lacked the courage to tell others about it, much less attempt to do it in front of them.

Upon noticing my cowardice on a day when there were no dolphins in sight, I decided to admit to my close friend swimming with me—who had not yet seen the dolphins— that I was going to call them to us so that she could enjoy the experience. When I then called the dolphins and they came fairly quickly, both my friend and I were astonished.

My friend still periodically puzzles over what happened that day, as she, like me, continues many years later to work on absorbing the reality of such a surreal and extraordinary reality.

This is how deeply we've been programmed by our culture not to believe in our power—based in quantum physics—to draw the things we desire to us through focused intention. Or if we do believe in our capacity to do this, it's often a guarded belief and one that most of us would prefer to keep private in order to avoid the judgment of others.

Yet as Marianne Williamson points out, the majority of people in our culture actually believe in the workings of quantum physics, but are afraid to openly admit it due to their fear of ridicule. In fact, she's noticed during her speaking tours that if a member of her audience mocks these possibilities, the crowd remains silent. But if two or more people stand up to defend them, the majority will come forth in support of these beliefs.

Unfortunately, our discomfort with claiming our power to influence the creation of good lives for ourselves results in our dropping out of participating in the process, which leaves us at the mercy of the randomness of chance. By contrast, believing that we can participate in manifesting our dreams is critical to keeping us interested and involved in the process of actively pulling good lives to ourselves and to others and the world.

Healing My Lack of Focus

Once I both understood and experienced the power of focusing actively on what I wanted, I realized how disempowering a lack of focus on my dreams had been in my life. I also realized that anytime I lacked a strong sense of what I wanted, the Universe didn't have any idea what to deliver and would consequently leave me languishing in the midst of wispy and unformed desires.

To remedy this, I made a concerted effort to heal my lack of focus on the life I wanted and to convert this weakness to a personal strength. I began by developing a new manifesting program based on the lessons the dolphins were teaching me, starting with clarity on what I wanted and how to get it.

I began to use this new program around the time I was finishing the first edition of this book in 1999 and succeeded in drawing a number of good things to the book—including a strong US publisher and three foreign publishing contracts. These book manifestations were accompanied by an increase in enjoyable clients; an award-winning column; my parenting book *(Parachutes for Parents)* becoming a bestseller; and additional income from expanded consulting, public speaking and teaching opportunities.

In addition, our family enjoyed more travel and bonding during special expeditions with family and friends, including five weeks in Europe with our teenagers and broad US travel. We then moved to a condo with views of the ocean and overlooking Honolulu. It was a perfect home and center for gatherings with family and friends during our kids' final years before college and during college summers. And, there was more!

These are all things I had put on my list of desires and had, over time, drawn many of them to me by using the insights I was learning from the dolphins. Before long, my life had gone from a pretty good place to unique levels of fulfillment, and I credited this improvement to my dolphin-inspired manifesting program that I have memorialized in an ebook titled *Manifest!* (See Note #10)

But the manifestation that showed up a few years later and surprised me the most was my current husband, Tommy, who I had heard was available at a time when I was feeling upbeat and ready for a relationship following my divorce.

We had enjoyed a brief crush on each other in junior high, so I already knew I was drawn to him. Then, after overhearing him sing harmony with a group of mutual friends enjoying a wedding party at the Honolulu Academy of Arts next door to my condo, I decided to consciously call him from my heart in the same way I had called the dolphins to me.

After I had done this on two separate walks, one along Waikiki Beach and the other circling Kapiʻolani Park, I felt a strong sense that we had linked on some level and that he would soon come into my life. Unknown to me, around that same time, while paddling his one-man canoe along Waikiki Beach, Tommy had also made a conscious decision that he was ready for a meaningful relationship. But when nothing happened to bring us closer for the next several months, I assumed I had misread the feeling that we had hooked and would connect.

In time, I even forgot about it and refocused on the essence of what I wanted: I wanted to fill the remainder of my life with a truly fulfilling relationship.

In fact, related to this, I had made a phone call from my parked car outside the Outrigger Canoe Club located on the Gold Coast at the far end of Waikiki to finalize arrangements with my friend from California to secure the condo she had found for me. My goal was to live in LA for six months in order to finish writing my script about the sonar threat to the cetaceans and their ocean home. I had also met someone in LA who I thought might be of interest, so I planned to use this time to see if he and I might be a match.

After ending my call, I headed into the Outrigger, where I was meeting my girlfriends for breakfast for the second morning in a row. Although three of us had enjoyed breakfast there the day before, the fourth had missed our gathering due to a delay in her flight from another island, so we were meeting again to include her in our cherished time together.

Because of my phone call, I was running late for this second breakfast, so I was rushing toward the Club's entrance when I ran into Tommy, who was dashing out of the Club at that exact moment. He was hurrying to work following his morning paddling workout, hustling—head down—to his car. We literally ran into each other outside the clubhouse entrance, causing both of us to startle as our hearts began to pound. Tommy wiped the spilled coffee from his shirt, as we gazed unabashedly into each other's eyes. When I looked into his, I saw both the eighth-grade boy I had noticed and liked so many years earlier and the mature man and grandfather standing before me. It felt oddly as though I had found my long-lost friend and he had found his.

We then broke our gaze to quickly catch up before exchanging emails. I called my friend while driving home to cancel the LA condo. This "chance" meeting with

Tommy led to a wonderful whirlwind courtship and our marriage within the next six months. Now, eighteen years later, he offers me the personal and professional partnership of my dreams and is clearly the love of my life and partner to my soul.

That clinched it.

I had been surprisingly slow to accept that the dolphins were able to converse with me and equally slow to accept that I could influence the manifestations in my life. But, when Tommy and I connected, I surrendered to the reality that I had been actively involved in making it happen. With this surrender, I also surrendered to the idea that conscious manifesting is possible and that I had successfully engaged in it. It was finally clear to me that my dolphin-inspired personal development and manifesting program was powerful! It had not only prepared me for my connection with Tommy; it had pulled it to me!

Following this ultimate manifestation, I committed to using my manifesting program on a daily basis, and when I keep that commitment, the fulfillment of my dreams expands exponentially. But, when I slow it down or stop, so do my results. The subsequent course of my life has perfectly matched my dedication to this program, which has included some rough patches during the times I let it slide, and great surges of "Big Magic" during the times I keep my promise to myself to engage in this energizing and magical program.

The key is to clearly select my dreams and to then focus solely on what I have selected, while strongly yearning for them—without worry or doubt—to come to me. Because it's a dolphin-inspired program, it's not only engagingly playful and fun to do, it's also a source of immediate pleasure, and is as joyful to do as its results!

Let yourself both yearn for and be drawn
by the magnetic pull of who or what you care
about and love.

CHAPTER 11

Manifesting Insight #3:
Show Up for Your Dreams

*Get on the path of your dreams and meet
them there.*

I was first made aware of the importance of showing up for my dreams when I turned away from my first opportunity to swim with wild dolphins in order to play tennis.

My next introduction to this idea came at a time after I had connected with the dolphins and had been swimming with them regularly for a few years. On this particular occasion, a pair of dolphins flanked me on both sides soon after I entered the water on a slightly overcast day that was devoid of the usual rays of sunlight streaking through the water. Although dolphins had never flanked me before, both remained firmly in their position, one on each side of my body as they escorted me out to sea. Although I initially felt uneasy about being confined between them, I soon realized it was a friendly gesture and was able to relax.

But, in time, I started to feel uneasy again, this time due to my concern that we might be going out too far, coupled with the lack of sun making the unlit and shadowy water feel a bit ominous. So, rather than continue to swim with my escorts, I dropped out and treaded water as the pair continued to swim toward the horizon where they soon met up with a group of other dolphins surrounding a very tiny, wobbly baby. As I watched, the baby attempted what looked like a first jump a few inches out of the water, revealing that I had likely just missed his or her birth. When the group then submerged to leave the area, I turned to head back to the beach and was shocked to see that I was not out as far as I had feared.

While absorbing the reality that I had likely missed this dolphin's birth—an event that was high on my list of dreams and one I had repeatedly requested—I promised myself I would be more awake and aware in the future. I would be more conscious about showing up for potentially rewarding experiences, rather than mindlessly and abruptly pulling out of them as I had just done and then suffering the painful angst of a lost opportunity.

Just Do It! Show up for Your Dreams

In spite of my promise to myself to show up for my dreams, yet another, even bigger, lesson on the importance of doing this followed several months later. I was swimming at Makua Beach when the idea came to me to play the same passing game with the Oʻahu dolphins that I had enjoyed with the Big Island dolphins. But since there were no leaves or other debris in the water to use for passing, I returned later that week with two maile leaf vines that I had twisted into an open, environmentally friendly lei. Because no dolphins were in view that day, I swam out about twenty yards to drop the lei in the water while broadcasting a message asking the dolphins to find it and bring it back to me.

Before long, a small group of dolphins showed up and swam in the area near me, but kept their distance, and none of them seemed to have found the lei. After about thirty minutes, I decided to get out of the water to warm up on the beach. Yet, the moment I reached the shore's edge and had removed my flippers and pulled my polar suit halfway off, I had one of my more unusual experiences with the dolphins.

While I stood at the shoreline with waves lapping at my shins, about five of the dolphins began to rise straight up and then down as they seemed to dance in a straight line toward me in single file. Once in front of me, each dolphin individually rose up to his waist and then slid back down before making a ninety-degree turn to the right. That dolphin would then proceed to swim parallel along the shoreline, while the next dolphin in line approached me to repeat the exact same routine. I had not previously seen the wild dolphins do anything that looked choreographed, as this did, so it caught my attention. I also had a strong impression that these dolphins had the lei, but if I wanted to see it, I would have to jump into the water again. It felt as if the dolphins were trying to lure me into "showing up" for this "dream" they had brought to me in response to my request for it.

As I stood paralyzed between my desire to see if the dolphins had the lei and my wanting to get warm, the dolphins continued to beckon me to join them. Yet, still looking for my usual assurance that they had the lei before I was willing to reenter the water, I stood planted in the sand watching for a glimpse of the leaves, rather than follow my urge to simply jump in.

I never surrendered to the dolphins' call to play that day. Yet the moment I finished pulling off my polar suit to get dry and head home, I was filled with regret. The ridiculousness of being in conflict about simply diving into something so potentially interesting and pleasant—but without a guarantee sticker—was apparent. Why would I put my heels down and stay planted in the face of an invitation for adventure and fun, when it's so much easier to just dive into unrestrained participation in a world filled with possibilities?

The absurdity of not making such a simple, positive choice made me painfully aware of how often I had done this and, in the process, had missed opportunities to enjoy new adventures; valued connections; or meet special friends. One of the hardest parts of letting these experiences escape me is that I will never know just what I missed, and I didn't want to be excluded from any more of life's banquet of possibilities. So I again vowed never to resist participating in the array of opportunities presented to me—whether small or large.

More Lessons on Showing Up

I thought I had learned my lesson and would no longer allow my periodic tendency to resist jumping into the fullness of life to keep me from being present for my dreams. But to my surprise, I still had more to learn.

In fact, another lesson on the topic of showing up for my dreams surfaced soon afterwards at a time when I was feeling rushed to meet my deadline for the first edition of this book. As a result of this pressure, I began to start my days with writing, rather than with my daily meditation and manifesting program.

On this particular morning, after skipping my routine, I sat at my desk and began to type. Suddenly, I felt a strong call from the dolphins to come to the beach to play. Although I was torn, I felt more compelled to work than play, so I ignored this unusually strong call. But, the call persisted, which added to my conflict, and so I spent the morning leaving my desk to put on a swimsuit under my tee shirt and shorts, then returning to the computer to type a few words before getting up to pack a snack, and then returning to the computer again. At one point, I even gathered my snorkeling gear from the closet and headed for the front door of my condo. But after opening the door, I shut it again and returned to my desk. At that point I noticed myself doing the indecision shuffle I sometimes do, so I stopped. By noon, a strong thought came to me that I had just missed the birth of a baby, something I had repeatedly asked the dolphins to show me. But, I continued to resist the call and stuck with my plan to complete the book.

About a week later when I went to the beach, the dolphins were there when I arrived and remained until I left. Yet the only encounter I had that day was with a mother and "auntie" presenting me with a baby I estimated to be about a week old and was very likely born the day I was resisting the call to show up at the beach. Again, I felt the pain of my resistance to diving into life's possibilities, especially since seeing a dolphin birth was something I would have loved to witness and have still not seen.

In addition to underscoring my need to show up for my dreams, it seemed the dolphins were also conveying to me that not even writing a book on dolphins—one that might evoke more human interest in preserving their lives—should stand in the way of my showing up for participating in the fullness of the play and joy of life, and certainly not for the birth of new life.

The lesson for me that day was a big one. And so, I made yet another vow to myself. This vow was to continue to pursue my goal of doing all I could to pull more love to my own heart and the heart of humanity and the world, but to do this while also fully participating in life's experiences—for what meaning does life have if we don't show up or take time to enjoy its magic?

Thankfully, the dolphins finally succeeded in teaching me that showing up to meet with our dreams along life's path is a critical key to the very essence of life and the joy it offers.

Life is a banquet, but you have to show up and fill your plate to enjoy its abundance.

CHAPTER 12

Insight #4: Be Consistently Attractive to Your Dreams

*Entice your dreams in the same way they
entice you.*

If we are to successfully entice the people and events we want to draw into our lives, we must learn to remain as consistently attractive to them as they are to us. I received my first inkling about the importance of this concept when the dolphins delayed their initial contact with my ex-husband, Tom, and me until we could make ourselves more appealing to them and a better match to their positive and playful energies.

Interestingly, it wasn't until the dolphins offered me another lesson on being attractive to my dreams that I realized its full significance. This second reminder came during a time when I was filled with anger over the commercialization of swimming with the dolphins that included busloads of visitors overpopulating the pristine and peaceful Makua Beach. My irritation was fueled by the insensitive way this surplus of swimmers was chasing after the dolphins, often bumping their way in front of others to get closer to them.

A Dolphin Lesson Tucked into a Scolding

On a day when I was feeling particularly annoyed by the chaos the dolphin chasers were bringing to the beach, my dolphin guide circled me several times with his eyes closed, clearly sending me a message that he was ignoring me that day. Next, I received an even stronger message that the dolphins could handle the visitors and didn't need my help. I was further assured that having people come to the beach, even if there were too many of them and they lacked good manners, offered the dolphins an opportunity to connect with people in a way that might influence them to be more caring of the planet and its residents.

Of equal importance, they didn't need people like me to feel angry on their behalf, since my anger was spewing hateful energy into their home and served only to infect the beach and world with its own offensiveness. This was the closest I had come to being scolded by the dolphins, and I felt appropriately embarrassed by the strength of their reprimand. When I later learned that the group in the water that day belonged to an organization to promote the protection of dolphins and whales in Japan—a country that still slaughters and eats them—I felt even more ashamed of my anger at them.

On another occasion, when I was struggling to calm my irritations over a different swarm of swimmers overtaking the beach, the dolphins gathered around me in a serious, silent mood. The message I received that day informed me that my urge to care about the dolphins was appreciated. But the part of me that got so upset with others provided absolutely no value to the dolphins or the world, and it certainly didn't reflect well on me. Moreover, my irritable energies were far less attractive to the dolphins than the poor manners of the innocently naive swimmers chasing after them.

I was further sent the message that if I would observe more carefully how the dolphins were responding to the tourists, I would see a model for handling difficult situations with more calm and grace. I would see, for example, that they might tease some of the chasers in order to wear them out, while ignoring others to help them see the futility of their approach. In short, they would design ways to gently handle these people individually and in accordance with their particular needs, just as they had done with me on so many occasions.

Following this message, I noticed a dolphin in front of me teasing an overzealous swimmer by going back to him repeatedly after short dashes of escape from his grasp. Since this was not the dolphins' usual response to chasing and grabbing, I assumed this playful game with the intrusive swimmer right in front of me was in part for my benefit, since I was being strenuously ignored that day as a result of my irritations getting the best of me.

The moment I understood his message regarding my annoyance being worse than the behavior of the overzealous swimmer, the playful dolphin, who was now six feet below me, eyed me in the way a quarterback might eye his receiver. He then released a large bubble from a distance that was perfectly coordinated with the speed of my forward motion for me to catch it. As the bubble traveled slowly upward at a perfect angle toward my destination, I reached out to carefully grasp it in my hands. I had seen a video of two young dolphins playing volleyball with one of these viscous and stable bubbles that rises slowly without popping, and I was hoping to bounce this one back to the dolphin who had sent it.

However, just as I reached for the bubble, the aggressive swimmer swam quickly in front of me and stuck his finger into the bubble to pop it. This was the first one of these large stable bubbles I had witnessed a wild dolphin blow, and after watching the man pop it, I was sorely challenged to hold onto the message I had just received about calming my anger. In the midst of my struggle, I was again gently reminded to send love, not the poison of anger, into the ocean, if not for my own sake, for the sake of the dolphins and their home.

This was helping me to understand that if I could figure out how to remain loving under all conditions, as the dolphins do, I would not only be attractive to my dreams but would also fulfill my soul's purpose of letting only love flow through and from me at all times. Moreover, if all of us would harness the intention to consistently send love instead of the negative energies we've grown so used to discharging into the world, we could rather easily bring the goodness we claim to want to our hearts and the planet.

Although we've heard this message before, we seem to think it's beyond our reach and thus don't earnestly try to achieve it. Yet not only do the dolphins succeed in realizing this goal of steady attractiveness a few miles from our shores, they make it look easy and fun—and clearly more rewarding and effective than humanity's mulish habit of collecting so much irritation and anger to send into the world.

A month later, I had an opportunity to use this lesson on the importance of preserving our attractiveness under considerably more challenging conditions. It took place during a weeklong workshop for swimmers new to the dolphin experience. Although I had spent many years in the water with cetaceans by then, I was attending this beginner's tour in order to spend time with a dear friend I had not seen in years.

I was shocked on our very first day by the insensitive behavior of the workshop leaders as they overswam their guests, literally swimming over their bodies to pass them. They would then dive into the middle of the various dolphin groups who had come to visit, consistently dispersing and scaring them off. Once all the dolphins were gone, our leaders would surface with wide grins filling their faces, proclaiming that the dolphins had invited them to swim in the middle of their pod.

Most of the beginners were taken in by these claims, but I was distressed by how often the leaders were spoiling good dolphin encounters for their workshop attendees by swimming *at* the dolphins instead of *alongside* them, and I was tempted to tattle to the person who had hired them, since I knew she would not approve. In the past, I would have allowed my irritation with this situation to destroy my own attractiveness enough to infect the other participants with my annoyance as well. But now I was aware that any anger I allowed to take hold in my heart would not only render me personally unattractive, but would likely repel the dolphins from being drawn to our group.

To hold onto my attractiveness, I spent much of that week in meditation and prayer, calling gentle feelings to rest in my heart in the midst of this annoying situation. Although I was sporadically rewarded for my success, the real prize came on the last day of the workshop, which was glorious from beginning to end. As the morning sunlight danced on the deep blue water, there loomed a bit of tension in our group as we collectively hoped for an even better day than the adequate ones we had enjoyed during our week together.

To our pleasant surprise, the moment we pulled out of the harbor, it appeared that all of the whales still remaining in the islands, prior to launching on their trip north, began to entertain us with full-bodied leaps into the air. I marveled at how many had come to play and at their defiance of the Newtonian laws of physics, as they repeatedly raised their forty-ton bodies all the way out of the ocean, with the help of only a single tail and a pair of spindly fins.

Later, when we arrived at one of the inlets along the shore, we found it filled with about sixty dolphins playing with a small group of gentle, respectful swimmers from another boat. But once again, our misbehaving leaders plunged themselves into the center of these groups, causing the dolphins to scatter and retreat. Once our leaders had again succeeded in chasing all the dolphins away, we were instructed to return to the boat in order to follow them.

As I swam slowly toward our boat, feeling reluctant about the plan to pursue the escaping dolphins, I came across our captain, who had spotted two manta rays on his way back to the boat and was now following them with his video camera in tow. Because he was the captain, I decided to follow along behind him, silently calling the rays to us from my heart. I was startled by their sharp U-turn in tandem, followed by their swimming directly toward us, and was glad I had spent the week meditating myself into a peacefully loving and attractive state.

The captain was also pleased and nodded to me as he pointed his camera at them with excitement. But our reverie was soon broken when one of the leaders emerged. He physically bumped into my shoulder as he rushed past me toward the rays, who immediately did a U-turn away from him before diving deep and escaping to safety. I too did a U-turn in the opposite direction to head for the boat, while working hard to quell my frustration.

On my way, I ran into a delightfully gentle woman from our group who invited me to join her to greet some dolphins she had spotted approaching our boat from the other side. Swimming side by side, we instinctively began to tone in unison into the water, as we called the dolphins to us from our hearts. We were soon surrounded by about twenty dolphins, who paraded in front of us in twos and threes, gazing, smiling, and caressing each other or "holding fins," as we were doing. An adorably wrinkly baby repeatedly showed off his new jumping skills as we cheered him on with our squeals of delight. I knew that some babies attempt to jump about two hours after birth, so calculated that these jumps were likely his first attempts. It felt like a great honor that his mother had let him come so close to us for his debut.

Next, three adults approached and engaged us in gazes and bursts of loving energy. Then the mother came by again, this time with her baby attached to her for nursing. I felt blessed to have enjoyed this final experience of joy for the week and was grateful to have learned to hold onto my peace and attractiveness, which I realized had drawn this experience to me.

Of even greater importance, when we returned to the boat, I noticed that a shift had taken place within my heart that had, at last, enabled me to feel softer and more loving toward the leaders. By consciously holding onto love, I had not only succeeded in being attractive to the mantas and dolphins, but I was finally starting to heal my heart and its ability to hold onto love for others, even under challenging conditions.

It became apparent that this would be a worthy goal for humanity: to feel this level of peacefulness and love in each other's presence no matter what conditions challenge us; to keep our hearts open no matter how others behave; and to send feelings of compassion and caring to everyone, under all circumstances. Collectively doing this would create more attractiveness for us all, which would, in turn, draw abundantly more good fortune from the Universe to humanity.

Be enticing to your dreams and a more loving world by cultivating a loving heart.

CHAPTER 13

Insight #5: Play While You Wait for Your Dreams to Arrive

Replace your vibrations of worry and stress with the upbeat and attractive energies of play.

Nothing is quite as self-defeating as selecting a dream we hope to fulfill and then repelling the dream by feeling glum and gloomy because it has not yet arrived.

Just as it's more charming to wait calmly for our restaurant orders to be prepared than to act edgy and ugly while waiting to be served, anytime a dream has been identified and called for, the best way to attract it is to be happy while you wait for its arrival. Although being cheerful can be harder when our dreams are slow to show up, anytime we fall prey to repellant worries and doubts about the timing of a dream's delivery, that dream—much like the dolphins—may no longer feel linked to us or drawn to be in our presence. Instead, it may unhook from us and elect to change course and go elsewhere.

So what else can we do besides fuss and worry while waiting for a dream to arrive? How can we successfully follow the dolphins' suggestion to maintain our happiness as we wait for a dream to find us and become a part of our lives, especially when it could take months or even a year or more for it to occur?

In order to maintain our allure to the dreams we've called to our lives, the dolphins suggest we play while we wait for them to appear. Not only does playing give us something pleasant to do, it boosts our mood in a way that ensures our attractiveness to the dreams we hope to entice. But of even greater importance, the true magic happens when our allure is so strong that it inspires the dreams we're calling to us to yearn for us as well.

The Value of Playing While We Wait

Because the art of play is one of the Higher Self traits that the dolphins so fully embody, they're able to carry the joy and attractiveness that the lightheartedness of play brings to them wherever they go. Not surprisingly, this is one of the primary ways the dolphins generate so much allure that they inspire a universal feeling of love for them, along with a strong desire in others to be near them.

Playing while we wait also ensures that we don't put off the joy of life or postpone our gratitude for what we already have as we wait for new goals to be met. Postponing pleasure trains us to appreciate play only as a periodic, often reward-based event, rather than an integral part of life to enjoy without reason, as the dolphins do.

Thus, rather than succumb to the repelling mindset of impatience or worry while we wait for our dreams to show up, we can protect our attractiveness by opting to jump into the pleasure of life before they arrive. This happier state also encourages appealing receptors to form within our hearts, which then pull and hook us up to the matching positive essence of the experiences we desire.

The dolphins' favorite method for engaging us in this essential lesson is to tease us as we wait for them to show up to play, usually to the point of prompting laughter at ourselves before they make a connection. More often than not, it's only after we've replaced our worries with the tickle and joy of our own laughter that the dolphins reward us by showing up in a state of glee. This teaches us how to allow the waiting period for the emergence of our dreams to be as joyful as the dream.

Relax, But Don't Surrender

Although the dolphins suggest we relax and play while waiting for our dreams to arrive, they also caution us to do this without surrendering the dream or letting go of our interest in it.

I initially assumed the instruction to relax and play while we wait was similar to the one taught by most other manifesting programs that encourage us to release and surrender our dreams to the Universe, or to God. But the dolphins have made it clear that this is not what they mean, since surrendering can be confused with giving up on our dreams and losing our interest in linking to them. Instead, their suggestion is that we actively hold our dreams in our hearts while also immersing ourselves in the pleasure of play as we wait.

This idea came into even clearer focus for me at a time when I was feeling discouraged as a writer. The dolphins—with their impeccable awareness and timing—used my malaise to reveal their fifth insight about playing without surrender.

I was driving out to Makua Beach, disquieted by several setbacks in my pursuit of a publisher, and I began to seriously consider that this might be a good time to release my dream of publishing a series of books designed to inspire my species to become a kinder and more loving humanity. In fact, I had gone far enough with my idea of surrendering this dream to have begun a search for golf and tennis communities, where I could enjoy more play while engaging in meditation and prayer as my contribution to the world.

In part, this was a sulky plan and a threat to God that I was ready to stop viewing my life as meaningful and intentional, unless the Universe would more actively support me in things like finding the right publisher. But it was also a genuinely attractive alternative to the agony and ecstasy of writing and publishing, and my threat was not altogether idle.

As I drove to the beach, I wondered if my discouragement would repel the dolphins, especially since encounters with them had become rare during the past year as a result of the rift among the humans in the beach community that had ultimately driven them away. When news of their disappearance spread, the beach got conspicuously less crowded, and the dolphins had only recently begun their return to Makua to offer periodic visits to the occasional beachgoer.

My hope was that I might be chosen for one of these rare encounters, but when I arrived, three swimmers were emerging from the water after completing their swim with a small group of dolphins, now lingering at the far end of the beach. Although I doubted the dolphins would return to the center of the beach to swim with me, I jumped into the ocean anyway. To my surprise, a dolphin established voice contact with me the moment I submerged my head under the water, raising my hopes of a swim after all. But the dolphins continued to remain quite a way down the beach from where I was swimming and where they usually joined people for connecting.

I felt let down, but pleased with the way I was gracefully yielding to the reality of not being approached for a reconnecting swim that day. Yet just as I was commending myself on my gracious surrender, I received a message that surrender was not the goal. And if I released my desire to reunite with my old friends after such a long separation, they would no longer feel as connected to me or drawn to the weakened energy of my non-yearning. At the same time, it was also important that I not fill myself with the angst of hurt or disappointment about not being chosen.

Although I understood the validity of this instruction, I was unclear about how to accomplish such a delicate balance between submitting to the attractiveness of contentment, while continuing to call my desire to swim with the dolphins to me. In short, I wasn't sure how to maintain my yearning for an encounter without engaging in the off-putting energies of attachment or feeling prematurely defeated by the growing evidence that it might not happen.

In the midst of my effort to figure this out, a strong message came through that I could simply play while I waited. This would keep my dream order active and alive, while maintaining my allure to the dolphins. In short, playing while I waited would put me into the desired state of a balance between yearning and feeling gratitude for what was already in my life, whereas trying to "let go"—or "surrender"—would have the effect of disconnecting me from the dream I desired. Moreover, since it was my dream, I needed to stay in the game—rather than hand it off to the Universe, or God, who didn't need to practice the art of manifesting. By staying in the game, I would not only be a participating cocreator, but I would also have a chance to practice my manifesting skills for drawing good to my life and the world.

After absorbing this message, I began to relax into my enjoyment of cooing to the fish and taking pleasure in the colors of the coral, while keeping my desire to swim with the dolphins actively purring in my heart. Within ten minutes the dolphins appeared for a visit that was filled with a mixture of quiet connections and frisky joy, and then they left. It was a short visit that felt somewhat aborted, but I elected to gracefully accept this brief encounter.

Then, to my surprise, I was gently chided for not learning the lesson I had just been taught. I was told to hold my focus on what I really wanted, while continuing to stay content without suffering because the dream had not yet been fully realized.

And so I did.

This time, the dolphins took longer to return, but as I waited, I again managed to hold onto my desire with a sense of lightness stirring in my heart as I hung out in gratitude with the fish and the colorful coral that were already there for me to enjoy and appreciate.

Eventually, the dolphins showed up for another encounter, in which about thirty of them played with me for an hour or more. During this time, they showed me a number of new experiences, some holding answers to questions I had formed before driving to the beach.

For example, in response to my query about how many dolphins join together to form what looks like a spinning triple- or quadruple-helix braid, four dolphins gathered carefully beneath me and got into position to do the spin. They amazed me by staying in that position while I counted how many were there, and just as I realized I was having trouble counting them, they amazed me again by breaking apart in slow motion and then into formation again, staying completely motionless while I more easily counted them. Then they enacted the spinning braid at half speed, allowing me to see just how they do it. I even managed to get some in-focus photos with my drugstore underwater camera of this normally fast-moving activity that I had not previously been able to capture on film.

Next, several pregnant mothers arrived and circled me several times. It occurred to me that this was significant in some way, and I wondered if I might be given a chance to witness a birth. Although there was no birth, a week later I learned that my own first grandchild had been conceived, so perhaps this abundance of pregnant mothers and babies was a prelude to our family's happy news. (Interestingly, several months later, those same dolphins spent an hour with that grandchild while he was still in his mother's womb during a time when she and my son came to visit and swim with them.)

Every time I thought my experience was complete, more dolphins showed up, some in pairs or threes, all moving in close to greet me. When this longer swim finally came to an end, I swam to shore exhausted and filled with gratitude.

Now I was genuinely satisfied and ready to say goodbye. Thus, rather than prematurely compel myself to "let go" of something I still desired as I had learned to do from other programs and was about to do, I had kept my dream energized, while playing as I waited, until it fully arrived.

I later realized that anytime I use the dolphins' tools in conjunction with other people also using them—as the dolphins do in their assemblages of anywhere from two to ten or more dolphins—the magnified energy of my group is able to generate even more vitality to our dreams and draw proportionately more goodness to our lives.

I was well aware of the potential of this kind of power, since I had experienced such strong doses of it whenever I was in the presence of the Oʻahu spinners during their morning meditative breathing together or when various groups of them were spinning and dancing across the water with the cadence of Sufi dancers, while squealing with joy.

But, the collective power of dolphins and whales was most explosively revealed to me during the times when I encountered superpods of a thousand or more—all aligned in positive energy and play—since the amplified power of so much joy generated by so many cetaceans is not just giddily contagious. It permeates everything. In fact, it was these encounters that led me to realize how inordinately powerful our human society could be if we would align ourselves in joyful groups yearning together to draw our loftiest dreams to ourselves, while we play as we wait for them to arrive.

Blending yearning with play while waiting for your dreams to show up creates the magic that will both connect and pull them to you.

CHAPTER 14

Benefitting from the Dolphins' Manifesting Insights

I believe in miracles.

The dolphins had taught me five unique insights for successful manifesting that were not only easier to follow than other programs, but also offered me far better results.

In the midst of enjoying my new success with the dolphins' unique manifesting program, I noticed how often my past dreams had not been well defined; nor had I stuck with them vigorously or long enough to fulfill them. In fact, I could see from the perspective of my new success that my prior weakness of attention to my dreams had been causing them to drift away from me.

Now I was learning to hold onto my yearning, while also remaining attractive to my dreams by playing while I waited for them to arrive. As a result of this shift in my approach to manifesting, my life and good fortune continued to improve, and even more good things began to draw to me.

The Benefits of My Manifesting Success

The most important of my manifestations was a new sense of peace and serenity within myself in addition to feeling more easily and consistently loving toward others. And, although I still had various issues and problems in my life, I seemed to be better able to handle them with calm effectiveness.

My career continued to flourish with even more parenting book sales taking *Parachutes for Parents* to best seller status; more delightful clients; and more parenting classes and other speaking opportunities, all contributing to my pleasure and success. My family was also blessed to move into a condo overlooking Honolulu and the ocean beyond during my kids' high school years as well as take a series of special family trips, including five exceptional weeks in Europe.

A surprising number of additional travel, career, and personal development opportunities surfaced following my even deeper immersion into my meditation and manifesting program after my kids had left for college—including attendance at two healing workshops that altered the course of my life. One of these was the life-changing experience of attending creator Francine Shapiro's first EMDR training in Hawai'i, which enabled me to heal the traumas I had experienced in my 20s, with aftershocks in my 30s and again in my early 40s. This was followed by my fortuitous attendance at the first public training given by Gary Craig, the innovator of Emotional Freedom Technique (EFT)—one of the most powerful of the trauma treatment programs—and later serving on his first board of directors.

Other random things seemed to unexpectedly draw to me, such as inspirational leader, Marianne Williamson, holding up my parenting book at one of her workshops I was attending in Hawai'i. She wanted to share a chapter from it with the Hawaiian leaders who had invited her to speak on how important their mediation method of Ho'oponopono (based on full transparency) is to bringing love and peace to the world.

We also went on magical sailing trips with friends in the San Juan Islands, the Caribbean, and Tonga, and I went with a friend to meet our daughters when their Semester at Sea ship ported in Hong Kong. These wonderful travels were capped by a special adventure with Jean Houston on a lecture cruise throughout her favorite Greek Isles.

Upon our return, we were invited to attend an excellent workshop given by John Gray at a private home in Hawai'i, where I met and befriended the delightful Cindie Black of Beyond Words, the first publisher of this book. Other serendipitous and special experiences like these had started to regularly draw to me, seemingly by magic and as a result of my daily commitment to doing my manifesting program that was keeping me attractively light and playful as I waited for good fortune to find me. And, it continued.

I began to realize from these rewarding results that my broadly sharing the dolphins' manifesting tips would be helpful to others wanting to create richer, fuller lives for themselves and a better life and world for us all. In preparation for sharing just how I did it, I sifted through the specific steps I believed had led to my success, and here's what I found.

A Recap of the Dolphins' Manifesting Steps

I had taken to heart the dolphins' first piece of advice to remain consistently attractive to my dreams at all times, and once I committed to this, I found it to be surprisingly easy to do.

I further committed to focusing only on the things I wanted to draw to me and to finally grasp the full importance of not allowing my fussing and worries or judgments of others to fill my head or heart, since giving these harmful energies my attention and focus would cause them to also be manifested.

I also finally absorbed the need to stick with the dreams I wanted to fulfill and to actively call them to me without letting go of this step or trying to hand it off to God, or spirit, to fulfill for me, as other programs had taught me to do.

Although each of these components was essential to my new program, the biggest change in my approach to manifesting was in learning how to actively pull my dreams to me by calling them from my heart, just as I had called the dolphins to me from the sea a few years earlier.

And, finally, I more firmly held onto the faith I had acquired as a child while fishing with my Dad, a faith that involved God and a baby baracuda swimming in the same waters as the dolphins I befriended forty years later. I share this full story in my ebook titled, *Manifest!*

Although I didn't initially grasp its importance, I had nevertheless noticed when I first called for the dolphins to come to me on that magical day that my yearning to connect with them felt like vibrating (even seeming to purr) deep in my chest. Interestingly, it was this vibrational humming of my heart—or the jiggling of a vibrational string within the structure of our vibrational universe—that seemed to serve as a conduit for reaching out and hooking me to the dolphins in order for me to then pull them to me with my continued yearning. I later realized that we're all vibrationally hooked to everything in our entangled universe, and that within this context we can select and yearn for the things we want more of in order to then pull them closer to us..

Of additional importance, during the time when I was calling the dolphins to me, I was also following their advice to be and feel playful while I waited. This additional step prevented me from feeling rebuffed or falling into discouragement or worry during the period of waiting that followed my request for the dolphins to come to me, and the time it took for them to arrive. As a result of this choice, life felt wonderful when the dolphins arrived. But, it also felt wonderful before they showed up.

Following this experience, I was more willing to know what I truly wanted and to actively send out vibrations of yearning to hook to those dreams and pull them to me. The reason for this new level of courage on my part is that dreaming for more of life's goodness no longer triggered fears that I might fail and be forced to endure the pain of being left out of life's bounty.

Once I fully understood and had experienced the dolphins' simple and playful approach to manifesting, it became an approach that was not only fun, but was also successful. And, so I continued to use it robustly.

My Next Dreams

In addition to the results I was already enjoying in my career, family life, and travel, I had recently identified some additional dreams I hoped to realize.

These new goals included having special experiences with the Australian dolphins and whales during the Sixth International Dolphin and Whale Conference I was scheduled to attend at Hervey Bay in southern Queensland. I also wanted to swim with the famed spotted dolphins off Bimini Island in the Bahamas and the humpback whales in the Silver Bank Whale Sanctuary off the Dominican Republic in the Caribbean. And finally, I wanted to pet the notoriously friendly gray whales in San Ignacio, Mexico.

Because I had already experienced so many years of cetacean encounters, I understood the potential for sitting in the middle of a vast ocean wondering where all the dolphins and whales had gone, an experience many people have after traveling long distances to see them. I realized that my dreams were not small and would need to manifest in short time frames due to our travel schedule. But with my new tools, I believed I could fulfill them. Following is my account of exactly what happened when I tested the five insights I had learned from the dolphins for consciously manifesting four specific dreams. (For clarification, I was still married to my first husband, Tom, at this time, so my references to Tom are to him, rather than to my current husband, also named Tom—but Tommy to me.)

The Jewel of Queensland's Crown, Australia

When I got to Hervey Bay in southern Queensland, Australia, I found their boat captains to be so effective in their respectful style of noncompetitive, alongside approaches to whale watching that I was not required to overcome any of the chaotic conditions I had encountered at the beach in Hawai'i. Nor did I need to argue with the captain, as I had on an American cruise in Mexico, in which the skippers of our smaller boats chased the gray whales hard enough to force them to make desperate, last-minute dives with their young calves in tow—and then exclaimed how special it was to see their tail flukes. Consequently, holding the dream of meeting with the whales happily in my heart was a good deal easier for me to accomplish in Australia, and doing so produced many wonderful experiences.

The only time I was even mildly challenged on this trip occurred during a whale-watching excursion that included among its passengers a king of one of the South African provinces, who had spoken on behalf of his country at the dolphin and whale conference. He was accompanied by his sister, her nine-year-old daughter, and a small group of other women dressed casually for whale-watching. There was also a more conservative Northern European group of passengers, all dressed in formal suits with ties, who were quite subdued and seemed uncomfortable with unreserved and playful activities.

After a rather quiet first hour without our odd mixture of people drawing any cetacean encounters to us, the young niece from the South African party, sitting next to me, began to plead with her mother to call to the whales. Her mother firmly shook her head no to each request, accompanied by a beseeching look that indicated the girl was not to ask again. But the girl persisted several more times. Then, giving up on her mother, she began to tap her hands on the outer side of our boat.

In spite of my awareness of the straight-laced group aboard, I thought of the dolphins' advice to play while we wait for our dreams to come true, so I encouraged this young girl's playfulness and joined her in tapping out a rhythm on the boat. Almost immediately, two whales produced a tandem spy-hop not far from our boat. And although most of the prim passengers continued to remain solemn, the girl and I began cheering louder and tapping faster as the whales drew closer.

When the girl again pleaded with her mother to call, her mother surrendered to her daughter's desire for play and opened her throat to release a most beautiful trill, similar to the one activist Joan Baez made famous in the sixties. Our two spy-hopping whales got very excited and responded with new, more vigorous and playful behaviors as they drew closer to our boat. Most of the solemn group began to relax and even smiled in appreciation of this joyful response, which was cut short by our need to return to the harbor. To my surprise, the whales followed us for quite a few miles as the woman continued to trill and our passengers relaxed and surrendered to the joy. This vignette graphically supports the dolphins' view that playing while we wait not only enhances our attractiveness, which pulls our dreams to us, but also teaches us how to experience more joy.

The Spotted Dolphins of Bimini in the Bahamas

I was later able to put the lesson about the importance of positive and playful energy to good use under more taxing conditions during my trip to Bimini in the Bahamas. Arrangements were in place for a short flight by seaplane to Bimini Island, where Tom and I would use a narrow, two-day window to connect with Bimini's famed spotted dolphins.

Yet as we were waiting to board our seaplane, we received a phone call indicating that things might be turning against us. The weather had gone bad in Bimini, and we were forced to cancel one of the days we were scheduled to be there, which narrowed our small window for meeting with the dolphins to only one afternoon. In addition, the boat owned by the people I had so carefully selected to serve as our escorts had been damaged enough in the storm to require being put on the blocks for repairs.

I could feel myself dive into my fear that things weren't going as needed for us to swim with the Bimini dolphins. But I caught myself mid dive and, rather than fall into the repelling trap of discouragement, I moved my awareness to my heart to call the dolphins to me. Focusing on my yearning instead of my fears not only lifted my spirits, but kept my attractiveness to the Bimini dolphins intact.

As I sat in the lobby waiting for our seaplane, while holding onto my positive thoughts, I noticed that right outside the window of the reception area was a dolphin in the waterway waving his tail at me. I blinked and took a second look at the waterway in time to see him wave his tail again. It seemed like a surreal experience to view this completely unexpected and humorous sight. In fact, I was so startled by the appearance of this lone dolphin in the narrow waterway that I went to the counter to ask if dolphins typically came into this area. The woman at the desk responded that an occasional dolphin might show up from time to time, but that it was a very rare event. When she then looked out the window to see what I was seeing, she was almost as surprised as I was to see this dolphin looking back at us.

Following this good omen, we received a call with the news that our contact on Bimini had arranged for us to go out with the only alternative boat and captain on the island, a person who also knew how to connect with the dolphins. However, they warned us that, unlike themselves, this captain did not believe in telepathic communication with the dolphins and would simply drive his boat to the area and hope for the best. Rather than fall into fear that this captain would not be as good as our original selection, once again, I held my focus on our goal to connect with the dolphins and stayed with it throughout our flight to the island.

When our seaplane touched down at Bimini, the wind was brisk and cold. No boats had gone out that day, and the villagers were uncharacteristically sporting sweaters and jackets. After touring the island and dining at a local restaurant, we bundled up to retire for the night. The temptation to feel discouraged continued to lurk in the shadows of my mind and heart, but I used the dolphins' advice once again and made a conscious choice to hold onto my positive focus, while keeping my energy light. As a result, I was able to drop off to sleep that night, successfully holding the famed spotted dolphins happily in my heart.

When we awoke the following day, the sun shone brightly through the cloudless sky on a calm blue ocean. Our captain launched his boat in the still, clear waters to begin our journey to the area where so many others had met with the illustrious Bimini dolphins. However, in the process of getting seated, Tom and I began to bicker, and I feared that our discord would interfere with the good fortune I sensed was coming toward us. So rather than get engaged in this senseless disagreement, as I often did, I separated myself from it and got quiet within. Before long, I was reconnected to my faith in good things happening for me, while sending Tom good wishes as well. Once settled, I calmly called the Bimini dolphins to our group.

With focus and faith again filling my heart with contentment, I felt myself begin to relax in the warm sun. My eyes closed lazily as I laid back against the bow of the boat and surrendered to my knowing that the dolphins were on their way, coming toward us as we went toward them. No further ripples of fear or doubt disturbed my confidence, and I rested peacefully in this faith for the next twenty minutes, while listening to the sounds of our boat gliding through the water.

I realized I was not only immersed in one of my favorite activities, but was now literally playing joyfully and without irritation, worry, or fear, while I waited for a connection with the spotted Biminis.

Suddenly, I was startled out of my reverie when I heard a voice call, "There they are!"

As I roused myself to look, I saw about thirty dolphins jumping and playing ahead of us. The skipper was surprised by how many dolphins were in the group and kept exclaiming that all three pods had joined together to greet us. He maneuvered his boat perfectly, providing a respectful distance between the dolphins and us, while steering on a course that was parallel to theirs. As a result of his skills, the dolphins soon bounded toward the boat and positioned themselves to play in both our bow and wake waves.

I could now see some spotted dolphins, as well as a few common bottlenose dolphins, including many adults, several adolescents, and a handful of babies among them. They seemed to be enjoying the waves our boat provided, so when the skipper began to slow down so we could stop and get in the water with them, I asked if he would be willing to continue to create these waves a bit longer as our gift to the dolphins.

When he disagreed with my plan and began to further cut his speed, I was challenged to hold onto my loving feelings while calmly sharing my belief that we would have a better experience if we offered the dolphins the gift of playing in our waves a bit longer. Although he was concerned that we might miss our chance to swim with these dolphins if we didn't grab it now, when I assured him we were willing to take that chance, he agreed to continue. We spent the next twenty minutes whooping and hollering, as the Bimini dolphins surfed and played in our bow and wake waves.

Then they stopped and milled around our boat, letting us know they were ready for a swim, a behavior I had seen on many occasions. As we prepared to enter the water, the skipper shared that these dolphins loved people to be as active and innovative as possible. And so we were challenged for the next hour to keep up with these delightfully playful dolphins.

When I first got into the water, it seemed as though all thirty dolphins instantly surrounded me, bumping into each other and me in order to get closer. I had never experienced such a cordial encounter and was thoroughly enjoying their exuberance. Then one of the dolphins stood upright before me for about a half a minute, as we exchanged bows and Namasté messages from the heart, each honoring the other.

The dolphins chirped and squeaked and swam toward us and beside us; they raced in circles around us; they brought grass and leaves for us to exchange with them; they invited us to dive with them; they held hands when we did; and they gathered below us all together, sending clicks of healing sonar up to us. When I asked if they would send a bubble, one instantly released a large one right to me. A second dolphin released another bubble when I thought about bubbles again. Another dolphin caught this bubble in his mouth and popped it. The more we dove, the more the dolphins liked it. Two dolphins did the double-helix spin beneath me, surprising me that they knew of my inquisitiveness about this activity. Others blew a burst of smaller bubbles, some jumped and somersaulted, and still others snuggled in pairs and threes as they gazed at us or tried to include us in their snuggling. About five babies played with us as a group, while their parents allowed them to get close enough to bump into us or snuggle. We were blasted until fully sated with these dolphins' welcoming spirit of love and unbridled joy.

And so we played and danced with these delightful dolphins until we were out of breath and could dance no more. Only then did these spotted dolphins say their goodbyes and begin to leave the area. Yet even after we had returned to the boat and had begun our trip back to shore, a number of them continued to follow us—some of them still jumping—as the skipper repeatedly expressed his amazement at the robust greeting we had received, the amount of time the dolphins had spent with us, and the unusual number of bubbles they had blown.

I was thankful I had employed the dolphins' manifesting tools for creating yet another exceptional experience and was beginning to feel increasingly more adept with using them. Little did I know how much I would need to draw from these tools in the next few days to overcome some uniquely challenging conditions we would face in the Caribbean on the coral shoals of the Silver Bank off the Dominican Republic. There I would seek to fulfill my dream of swimming with whales for the first time.

The Silver Bank Whales of the Caribbean

After swimming with dolphins, which are technically small whales, I developed a growing desire to swim with the larger humpbacks. So I arranged a trip to the world's largest humpback birthing and calving nursery on the Silver Bank off the coast of the Dominican Republic in the Caribbean.

Getting to the Silver Bank was not easy, nor did I find it an adventure for wimps. After several long flights to get to Puerto Plata in the Dominican Republic, Tom and I discovered that we were the oldest couple to board the boat that would serve as our home for a week on the Silver Bank. The boat ran all night, enabling us to awaken the next morning to a beautiful sunrise and breakfast.

However, tensions started soon after breakfast, as people maneuvered to be placed with the most compatible group and the best captain. We had been told that our two groups of visitors would remain fixed for the week, once formed, but would alternate between the two small tender boats and their captains, who would get us closer to the whales than the mother boat could manage.

The group we were assigned to was filled with professionals who were individually engaging, but our collection of egos began to clash early in the day as we jockeyed for the best gear and seats on the boat—a clash that didn't enhance our attractiveness to the whales. As a result of our group's disharmony, our first day in search of whales produced no encounters, in stark contrast to a fulfilling swim with a group of dolphins and two whales reported over dinner by the easygoing group with the more congenial captain.

To add to the disappointment of not seeing any whales, my transfer from our tender boat back to the mother boat went seriously wrong: I was dropped into the rough water between the two boats as they slammed back and forth at each other in the choppy waters. Gratefully, I fell between the slams and was able to dive beneath the tender boat in the same manner I had learned to dive under large waves while bodysurfing as a kid growing up in Hawai'i. Relieved to have survived such a close call with only a wrenched shoulder, I was determined to continue with my plan to swim with the whales in spite of my injury. As it turned out, it was a good thing that my fortitude and focus were so strong, since there were even more distractions that vied for my attention throughout the next day.

After our group had been so completely ignored by the Silver Bank whales that first day, hearing about the good fortune of the other group caused us to feel even more anxious about our inability to attract whales. At dinner that evening, I could sense the tensions rising as we each secretly blamed the others for our failure, mixed with fragile hopes to do better the next day. To deal with my own concerns about being part of the rejected group, I spent time while dropping off to sleep that night yearning from my heart to pull some whale calves and their mothers to me the next day, in spite of the conditions.

Fortunately, the more congenial captain of the alternate boat was able to get our group to relax a bit, which drew two whales to spyhop fairly close to our boat, finally uniting us in relief and joy. Now drawn to our group's more integrated energy, the whales came even closer to our boat to give us a dramatic breaching show to the accompaniment of our grateful hoots and hollers.

Not long after this show, we received a call from the other boat inviting us to join them in a special interaction they were having with a mother whale and her calf. We arrived to see the mother floating twenty feet beneath the surface on her back, with her pectoral fins outstretched to the sky in an open gesture, as if to welcome us into her heart and home. We slipped into the water.

It was a moment of great majesty, and I was overcome with tears as I floated above this noble whale with my head bowed and hands clasped to my heart. I floated there for the next half hour, mesmerized, as she remained in this ecstatic pose, her calf mimicking it from beneath her while peeking out at the people from time to time. Her escort stayed quietly nearby, watching us closely as he patiently indulged this mother whale in her kindness to the people.

Finally, this kind whale ended her hour-long encounter with the visiting humans by slowly turning to her side, careful not to hit any swimmers or catch them in her slipstream, as she attentively fluttered her forty feet of whale tonnage away from us. Although I had initially felt some fear about swimming with a whale that size, my pounding heart was quickly calmed by this special whale's gentle and welcoming energy.

Even though our group was more relaxed following this magnificent experience, a growing sense that the other group was better at attracting whales than ours could not be overlooked, and we began to feel like the losers in an undeclared and invisible competition. The more playful captain inadvertently contributed to our growing fears by lightheartedly asking who in our group was "causing the problem."

Not surprisingly, the lack of group attractiveness resulting from so much tension continued to affect our encounters. And, although we enjoyed a number of topside shows over the next few days, I experienced only one underwater encounter, albeit a wonderful experience of gazing into a humpback whale calf's eyes for a few moments.

On our final day at the Silver Bank Sanctuary, I decided to release my goal of creating group synergy and branch out on my own to focus on manifesting more underwater encounters. By releasing the group, I was better able to focus on the tools the dolphins had taught me and started with finding a way to be more personally attractive to the whales. I did this by releasing the collective worries and doubts of our group and actively filling my own heart with love. I then focused only on drawing whales to me, rather than dwell on my doubts about whether or not this was possible under the circumstances of our group's tensions.

Before long, a series of whales began to approach our boat. When they showed up, I showed up as well—in alignment with the dolphins' lesson about "showing up for our dreams." Our captains had tried all week to persuade our group to get into the water as soon as the whales approached us, but we had all been slow to respond. Now, due to my clearer intention to individually connect with the whales, I got into the water more quickly than I had when I was trying to merge with my group.

Once in the water, I found myself all alone, face-to-face with a 25 ton mother and her sizable calf (the length of two basketball players and weighing about a ton). They were swimming so close to me that my heart began to race as I adjusted to their size and proximity to me. Next, a second mother swam slowly by with her calf, floppily riding on her back while staring into my eyes with a soulful gaze. A third and final mother let her calf swim between us to give him a closer look at the human visiting his nursery. And to end the show, a male escort swimming just ten feet below me looked enough like a gliding building to make my heart catch in amazement and then race with fear.

Following this series of breathtaking encounters, I was sitting on our pontoon feeling fully sated when we heard a whale singing so loudly that we could hear his song without the aid of hydrophones. When I slipped into the water to make my own tonal sounds in response to his, the whale mimicked each sound I made and then waited for my next one, just as the humpbacks in Hawai'i had done with me through the hydrophones our captain had placed in the water. This went on for a few minutes, as the whale drew closer and closer, until it occurred to me that he seemed so close I was surprised I couldn't see him.

I put my head up to ask if the young doctor who had joined me in the water knew where he was. I then looked to the left where the doctor was looking and saw the whale's tail thrust very high out of the water, waving back and forth as though he was not just answering my question, but was now teasing us.

When the whale slipped beneath the surface again, the two of us submerged our heads under the water to join him. He then made a shift from the high, short tones he had been exchanging with me to a longer, very deep and reverberating sound. The vibration from this singular low tone hit both the doctor and me with such a paralyzing force to our lungs that we weren't able to breathe for what seemed like an eternity.

The moment the sound finally stopped and our lungs were released, we each broke through the water, simultaneously exclaiming, "Did you feel that?!" We both then put our heads down at once and began to swim as fast as possible back to our boat, where we quickly scrambled onto it and out of the reach of this unpredictable whale.

Once safely back on our pontoon, we looked for the whale and saw his head surface about ten feet from our small boat, looking as if he was preparing to ram us. But instead, he stopped to make eye contact with me before sending a surge of loving energy equal in strength to the blast he had sent earlier to my lungs. The whale then dove, but rather than complete his dive, he stopped short, with most of his body still above the water and his tail pointing to the sky like an exclamation mark. He remained in that position for a full minute, causing me to wonder how he was able to hold himself so high out of the water for so long. Next, he waved his tail back and forth from this high position for another thirty seconds, before sinking into the ocean to complete his dive and his farewell.

Not only had this whale made it clear that if he had sent a slightly stronger blast of his sonar he could have exploded our lungs, he also impressed on my mind that this is what the power of sonar is capable of doing and is what is killing his family. As an activist involved with a group of other activists concerned about the screeching sounds of the sonar bothering the whales with the intensity of its noise, I immediately grasped from this whale that the sonar problem was a good deal more dangerous than our small group had concluded. I now understood that the sonar was not just a nuisance for the cetaceans but had the capacity to kill them.

Although the shoulder injury resulting from my fall a few days earlier had been growing steadily worse, following our time with the singing whale, I was completely pain-free and never noticed my shoulder again. I was also drenched in euphoria as I returned to the boat, in spite of initially having feared for my life during the whale's blast of sonar to my lungs.

As the young doctor and I pulled ourselves back onto the boat, I noticed that the rest of our group had finally put on their gear and were ready to slip into the water. Their lateness to get mobilized and thus missing the whale reminded me of the Hawai'i dolphins' lesson about the importance of showing up for your dreams. This remarkable day had shown me how well it works not only to hold your dreams actively in your heart, but to then show up for them when they arrive.

On our way back to the mother boat, I was still processing the importance of my experience with the singing whale when our boat came upon a group of dolphins playing with several whales. As we approached this group, the dolphins surrounded our boat and then slowed down to invite us into the water. It was the perfect ending, since everyone on our boat, now at last feeling calmer and closer to one another, showed up in time to participate as a group in this playful finale.

On that last night before our departure, a number of whales drew near our mother boat at sunset, offering repeated, multiple waves goodbye with both their pectoral fins and tails waving back and forth. I marveled once again at the conscious nature of cetaceans and smiled at the success of this trip and my growing skills in manifesting my dreams.

The "Friendlies" of Mexico's San Ignacio Lagoon

Our first evening in San Ignacio, the beautiful Mexican whale nursery, was stunning. The lagoon was filled with multiple shades of turquoise, lavender, heliotrope, and blue, offset by white birds flying against the backdrop of pale yellow mountains and a luminous moon. The sun set in oranges and reds over our pristine outhouses, rustic tents, and bags of shower water "warming" in the cool evening sun. Nobody complained of our conditions, and only the sounds of oohs and aahs between the clicks of cameras could be heard.

The following morning, we set out early in our rubber *panga* fishing boats steered by Mexican guides to meet with the famed and friendly San Ignacio gray whales, nicknamed by the Mexican locals as *las amistosas*, or "the friendlies." We found ourselves in a six-person panga, amidst only twelve other pangas allowed on the lagoon at any one time. The passengers in these boats had all traveled from afar for a special whale experience, and our collective hopes and worries were mounting.

Our panga was filled with a successful and genteel businessman, his beautiful veterinarian wife, a healthcare worker, and her elderly, ill mother, who had sneaked out of town without her doctor's permission in order to kiss a whale before she died. It seemed the whales were everywhere in the lagoon, yet they were eluding the boats. A sense of worry began to fill the air. I noted with disappointment that some of the famously skilled Mexican boatmen were chasing the whales, and I felt dismay that commercialism was infecting their usually respectful and effective approach.

I quickly released my pique over this behavior, while the other lovely and harmonious people on our boat began to relax and chat among themselves. Upon learning that the veterinarian also believed in animal telepathy and used it in her practice, I was reminded to consciously put my focus in my heart as I telepathically called the whales to us. Before long, I could feel that I was in the right emotional state for attracting the whales to our boat, mixed with a strong faith that they would come. This time it had taken only a few moments to release my annoyance with the commercialism infecting this special place and to reach my harmoniously focused and faithful state. I noted with gratitude that the dolphins' tools were finally becoming second nature to me.

Before long, a gray mother whale and her calf—both marked by nature with a white, iris-shaped star—surfaced about six feet from the bow of our boat, where I was sitting. It surprised me when the two of them then popped up together in a dual spy-hop to check out our group, followed by the calf drawing even closer to us as he continued to spy-hop by himself. He then began to flirt with our group by rolling over playfully on his side, and his mother soon joined him to also play with us for the next half hour.

Our particular boatman knew how to quietly approach the whales while keeping a respectful distance. Then, whenever the whales got close to us, he would stop, keeping his engine idling, which allowed them to keep auditory tabs on our position and safely approach to the degree they desired.

I began to send even stronger waves of love from my heart toward this mother and her calf, while yearning for them to draw near enough for me to touch and pet them. The calf slowly moved closer and closer, while watching me carefully, before retreating a bit and then drawing closer again. In the midst of this calf working up his courage to let me pet him, his mother would periodically give him a nudge toward me, while I continued to hold firm to the magnetic connection I had created between us.

Eventually, the calf made his way to the bow of our boat, where he remained under the water beneath me with his head shyly bowed toward his lagoon's sandy floor. I gazed intently at the top of his head, as I pulled it toward me with the vibrational yearning of my heart. I could feel the magnetism between us strengthen as the calf's head began to slowly rise, as if in slow motion, up and out of the water until it reached my waiting hand, then paused as I caressed his surprisingly velvety crown.

He then submerged himself again before raising his head even further out of the water until it reached my face, which was now hanging over the bow to greet and kiss him. Once again, I thought of the idea that "What you yearn for also yearns for you," as I continued to pet and kiss this calf who seemed as interested in my love as I was in his. He repeated this gesture several times and was soon joined by his mother.

Our group played for about an hour with Iris, as we later named the mother, and her adorable calf. Our guide noted that he had seen this mother and calf pair earlier in the season but had never seen them approach a boat for even minimal interactions, much less petting, hugging, and kissing.

I petted many more whales that week, saw multiple breaches and bubbles, witnessed the elderly woman kiss her whale, and even had a whale mischievously blow a snout full of water at me. But, this first encounter with Iris and her calf was special, in part due to my participation in pulling them to me with the help of the dolphins' manifesting tools.

Upon my return home to Hawai'i, I thought of how wonderful our society and world could be if we used our children's time at school to teach them such things as the dolphins' insights for being their best selves and how to manifest a life and world of their dreams.

A golden heart, a golden life.

CHAPTER 15

Insight #6: Jump Just for the Joy of It!

Jump for the joy of it to protect your freedom to be your authentic self. And, if you've lost that freedom, jump for the joy of it to protect your spirit.

Upon returning home from my satisfying trips, I jumped back into the busyness of my life, and before long, the part of each morning I dedicate to my program of focusing on manifesting my goals had become brief, if I fit it in at all. As a result, I spent little or no time attending to my dreams, and not surprisingly, they weren't manifesting as well as they had done during my trips.

Because the next dreams on my list were both big and important to me, I made yet another one of my vows. This time I vowed to do at least thirty minutes every day of some form of my manifesting program described in the previous chapter (14) and in my ebook titled, *Manifest!* Whenever I gave even more time to this key part of each day, my life was empowered, but when I kept it short or broke my promise to myself, I experienced a perceptible reduction in the manifestations of my dreams. Noticing this pendulum of power swinging back and forth in accordance with my dedication to the program, I recommitted to doing the full program each day.

This resulted in my attracting a strong publisher, a goal that had been at the top of my list. But when I saw this publisher's contract, offering me almost no benefits at all, I found myself in a catch 22 paradox. I was excited about being approached by such a strong publisher for the first edition of this book; yet I was also uncertain about how to respond to the weakness of their proposal. Although the publisher was large in both size and stature, their offer seemed unduly meager if not unkind, which raised my concerns about entering into such an inequitable partnership. Yet it was also hard to let the offer go, and I fell into confusion.

When I couldn't find a clear answer to this dilemma in my manifesting tools, I drove to the beach to ask if the dolphins had an opinion on what I should do. Even though I had not previously initiated requests for their opinions and understood that they aren't fortunetellers, I thought they might like to weigh in, since the book was about them and their lessons for humanity,

But, rather than offer me a simple answer, the dolphins presented me with yet another insight. Initially, this insight was confusing to me, but in time I was able to grasp the wonderful subtleties of its full meaning and was struck by the overarching power it offered me personally and offers all of humanity.

The Dolphins Present Their Sixth Insight:

Jump for the Joy of it!

The core of this sixth and final insight is this: Jump for the joy of it! Although I didn't notice the distinction at first blush, there are two separate messages folded into this insight, each of them profound and vitally important to our lives.

The first of these messages is to "Jump for the joy of being fully free to act as your authentic self, while also being mindful about using that freedom the moment it's threatened to vigorously protect it and to also help protect the freedom of others."

The second part of the message is to "jump for joy— even if you've lost your physical freedom—in order to protect your spirit as the last bastion of your liberty." This powerful insight was presented to me in the following way.

When I arrived at the beach to pose my question about my publishing contract, I was drawn to the cliff, where I instantly noticed about twenty dorsal fins bobbing in the water below where I often parked. Because I had never seen the sight of bobbing dorsal fins before, I quickly parked and got out of the car to set up my beach chair, while asking my question before even sitting down. Just as I was settling into my chair, a dolphin leaped a dramatic ten feet into the air, while sending a stronger-than-usual message to "jump for joy."

Although I was delighted by this quick response, the message didn't make sense to me; yet as I was mulling over what it might possibly mean, the dolphin repeated his leap into the air. But, this time, his leap was accompanied by a strongly transmitted message for me to "write the book just for the joy of it." With a shiver, I suddenly understood.

I had often nagged the lagoon dolphins to jump for joy, as they had done while living free in the ocean before their capture. Once in captivity, they had of course been conditioned to jump for rewards, but I felt certain that if they could recapture their taste for naturally jumping, just for the joy of it as they had done while in the wild, they would feel more like their authentic selves and be happier, even while in captivity.

Then one day at the lagoon, in response to my repeated suggestion about jumping for the joy of it, Keola startled me by leaping out of the water and then landing with a belly flop next to where I was standing. It was shocking to see a captive dolphin jumping between shows just for the joy of it, coupled with his claiming the freedom to do a belly flop similar to those I had so often seen in the wild. The moment Keola surfaced from his belly flop, he looked at me and I looked back at him, both of us grinning, yet stunned. It seemed as though each of us was as startled as the other by his jump and belly flop, and I threw my head back and began to laugh. Keola held his twinkling eye contact with me as he studied my face. It appeared that Keola was enjoying both my laughter and my understanding of what had just happened.

Now as I sat on the cliff, the wild dolphins were amusingly offering me the same suggestion I had offered Keola, but this time in the context of writing and selling my book as my authentic self, without compromise or concern for my reward. It seemed they were urging me to write the book not with my eye on the prominence of my publisher or how fair my royalty would be, but simply for the joy of writing it in the manner I believed it should be done.

Suddenly, I could see both the humor and wisdom of this idea and called out to the dolphins bobbing below me, "I get it!" I then laughed aloud at their ironic humor and delightful sixth insight about the importance of "jumping just for the joy of it" as a way to freely claim who I truly am at all times, regardless of whether I would be admired or rewarded.

This sixth insight "to jump just for the joy of it" helped me to realize that if I could recapture my childhood feelings of freedom to be my true self—just as I had coaxed the lagoon dolphins to do—I would be liberated to write my books openly and honestly for no reason other than the joy and freedom I first felt when I became a writer. That freedom included the most important freedom of all for me as an author, the freedom to passionately share my new, often controversial ideas for living life more clearly and kindly and with great joy. My heart stirred with excitement as I absorbed this permission to liberate my voice and my real self.

More Choices, More Learning

Now, focused more fully on the true purpose of my authorship and books than on my reward or what it might say about my worth, I accepted the small fee in order to secure an audience for the cetaceans' stories. This shift in my perception from my reward to telling their story freed me to feel as if I could jump just for the joy of it! And the next weeks were filled with free, fluid writing, simply because I love to write about such things as the dolphins' and whales' lessons and their survival story—and ours.

Then my final contract arrived, filled with new clues that I would most likely be discounted even more than I had thought, including the possibility of the book falling into limbo for years—or never getting published. When my questions and counteroffers were met with scorn, the arrangement began to feel unduly callous and out of balance. It was also growing chillingly clear that I would be giving up big chunks of my personal freedom if I signed.

Although I understood that the publisher was merely acting in accordance with what had become the standard publishing approach with non-celebrity authors, I wasn't used to such unequal status in my relationships with others. Yet it was hard to let go of such a good publisher, and I could see why people were reluctant to do it. I could also see why people fail to protect their freedom in advance by not walking away from these kinds of unequal partnerships. And so I continued to struggle with my decision.

More to the Sixth Insight than I Had Realized

The following day, I went back to the beach to see what more the dolphins might have to say on the subject. When I arrived, they were again waiting at the cliff. But this time their energy was solemn and there were no jumps of joy. Another strongly delivered message indicated that jumping for joy is natural and easy whenever you are free to authentically be who you truly are. But although it can still be done, it's considerably more challenging to do, once you have lost your freedom to express yourself fully and freely. Thus, even when it's hard, it's always better to protect your

equality and freedom in advance—whenever possible—
and before it's too late.

This was the most complex and profound thought the
dolphins had ever shared with me, and it constituted a subtle yet important message. It showed how humans can keep
their freedom if they're awake to its importance and willing
to muster their courage to protect it, rather than allow it to
be silently and steadily carved away from them while they
slumber or find it too hard to stand up to protect it.

With a jolt, I realized this had been an issue for me
throughout my life, as a woman born in the forties. I had
been taught to put my true self aside in favor of the narrow
freedoms allotted to women of my era—which, in spite of
some improvement, are still far too narrow for women today.
As a result, the dolphins' message for me to do everything
possible to protect my freedom—and my equality—struck a
deep chord in me, and I realized how true this is for all of us.

As fate would have it, I went to hear Marianne Williamson speak that evening on this very topic, and, to a standing
ovation, she encouraged disdained and marginalized people
to stop putting up with the unfair terms they're offered by
their society. As I listened, I wondered why we don't stand
up for ourselves, or for others, and I wanted to raise my
hand to ask why we don't do this.

As if to answer my unspoken question, Marianne
declared that we don't lack a nation of people with good
values or a sense of fairness; we lack a nation of people
with the courage to stand up for what we know to be right.
She then said something profound that caught my attention.

She explained that in order to stand up for equal and
fair relationships and partnerships for ourselves and

others, we must first let go of our enduring willingness to succumb to the dominance, greed, corruption, and cruelty of unkind people with a propensity to discount and dominate us.

Just as the dolphins had cautioned me earlier that day, Marianne Williamson told her audience that we must wake up in time to protect our freedom before it's too late! As I reflected on the importance of this dual warning, I could see why the dolphins had depicted the elation our preserved freedom inspires as the urge to jump for joy!

Finding Our Courage

Upon returning home that night, I thought of my unequal publishing contract and realized how perfectly the dolphins' message had hit the mark. It was clear that I would be wise to walk away from such an unequal partnership—even if it meant giving up a strong publisher—in order to protect my freedom to be my true self.

But I could also see why people don't do it. I knew it would be hard for me to walk away from such a prominent publisher, just as it's a challenge for people to leave the conditions that bind them to subservient lives or unfulfilling partnerships. Yet I also realized that as afraid as we may be to claim equality in our relationships and lives, it's even more terrifying to sign up for our own captivity.

The contrast between maintaining our freedom to be our true selves and losing it hit me. I could already see significant losses of freedom erupting throughout my own society and around the world, and it was indeed terrifying. I made the decision to face my fears and arrange for my own freedom and personal equality as an author and individual in all of my relationships—and to do so without indignation or anger, as the dolphins had taught me, but to simply do it.

And so I set out the following day to decline the unsatisfactory publishing contract and to either find a more equal partnership or publish the book myself. After doing this, I felt free to finish writing my book simply for the joy of it and with the freedom to add things to the book the publisher had not wanted to include.

Claiming my freedom to be my own self and live a life of my own choosing, served as a wake-up call for me! I realized the urgency and importance of this sixth and last dolphin insight for me personally and for every member of my society.

Selecting My Next Dream

I was ready to celebrate my personal courage and my freedom from the publisher's constraints, so I responded to a call to play with the dolphins. As I drove to the beach, I noticed that I had no further fears about negotiating contracts, now that I knew how to claim the truth of my desire for personal freedom and equality.

When I arrived, I saw dolphins playing on the surface well beyond the beach and cliff, so I drove in that direction. Then I lost sight of them but found a place to park along the side of the road. After getting tucked into this small spot, I glanced at the ocean just as two young dolphins rose in perfect synchronization out of the water and then arched their heads back to pull themselves into a rare and beautiful dual backflip. This was the second backflip I had seen in my decade of hanging out with dolphins and the first one in tandem.

While watching this display of strong harmony between the two dolphins, I became acutely aware that all of the feelings of smallness and fear I had experienced as an unknown author in the daunting world of publishing were gone. I felt peacefully aligned with the harmony the dolphins were reflecting for me and sensed a compatible publishing arrangement was on its way.

Sitting in my car absorbing the experience, I noticed the dolphins heading toward the beach, so I drove in that direction to go for a swim. When I got into the water, a young dolphin established immediate and constant voice contact with me. I sent out my "Yee-ha" signature sound of joy, which I thought I heard him mimic. Because none of the dolphins had ever copied this sound during my ten years of sending it into the water to greet them, I questioned if I had heard him correctly. Then he did it several more times, now more slowly and deliberately, echoing the sound of my joy back to me.

Next, I had a special encounter with my closest dolphin friends, who had served as my teachers for the past decade. To begin, three of them huddled together to do the energetic and empowering triple-helix spin under me. Following this, a mother with her tiny baby, only a day or two old, swam alongside me for a few minutes. At first, the baby peeked at me from behind his mother and then darted back to hide behind her again, followed by another longer peek until his peeks got long enough for us to gaze at each other for a moment. This was something I had not previously experienced, and I noticed that I was flooding with a mixture of gratitude and joy.

I didn't know at the time that this would be one of my last regular swims with the Hawai'i dolphins. My book project was coming to an end and so were their regular tutorials. As I said my goodbyes, I thanked the dolphins for this sixth insight, which had prompted me to reject the inequitable contract and take back my personal freedom to live as my true self before it would be too late. As I drove home, I not only felt lighter and freer, but as though I could jump for the joy of it.

New Pathways Open

When I returned home, I learned that the editor working for the strong publisher who had discovered and liked my book was leaving that publisher to move to another house. As it turned out, accepting the publisher's offer could have put my book in serious jeopardy, since nobody else there knew anything about the book or me.

I finished the bulk of the book within a week and went to visit the hotel dolphins, whom I had neglected during this final writing process.

Kaiko'o—the only captive dolphin to have responded to my suggestion to jump for the joy of it by jumping in the lagoon—seemed to discern that the wild dolphins had given me the same message I had given to him. He swam right over to me the moment I arrived and, looking very pleased with himself, sat upright before me and shuddered. Then, he dove to the bottom of the lagoon to get a rock, which he held proudly in his mouth while continuing to stand upright before me for a long, twinkly-eyed gaze as visitors snapped pictures of him.

Maka also gave me his attention that day, strutting by with a leaf on his tail, as did Iwa's son, Hoku, who had recently moved to the lagoon. I was enchanted by long periods of gazing into the eyes of each of them, which seemed more strongly connected to their hearts than usual. All three dolphins then swirled vortexes through the water with their fins and tails and blew a variety of bubbles.

Just as I was preparing to leave, Maka jumped three-quarters of the way out of the lagoon and then came over to bask in my squeals of amazement over his first "jump for joy." A few moments later, Hoku executed the same three-quarter jump. I was astonished that both of these dolphins, whom I had never seen do a free jump in their lagoon, each did one that particular day.

As I pondered why they had each decided to jump, I wondered if they had tuned into the conversation about "jumping just for the joy of it" and were possibly congratulating me for my courage to secure the freedom for myself that they had not been able to secure for themselves. I also wondered if they were acting on the second part of the "jump for the joy of it to preserve your spirit" part of the message given to me by the still wild part of their family, swimming free in the ocean just forty miles from their lagoon.

When I looked out at the hotel's beach, I noticed the waves lapping on its shore. I thought of the Makua Beach dolphins periodically swimming to Waikiki just a few miles away from this hotel's beach and wondered if they ever talked directly to these lagoon dolphins. It was a day filled with mystery and joy, and I felt deep gratitude for my decade-long journey with the wonderfully wise and kindly generous dolphins and whales.

Another Dream Arrives

A month later, I was nearing the end of editing my book and pulling it together to go to press. Three medium-sized publishers had shown interest in it, but none had followed up, and I was within a few weeks of starting the process of self-publishing. I was using my manifesting program on a daily basis, which resulted in my feeling peacefully confident that the best outcome for the book was on its way.

Before long, one of the medium-sized publishers contacted me, followed by a call from one of the other ones, and within a week, I signed a contract that offered me a fair publishing partnership. I had not only succeeded in preserving my freedom to act as my authentic self, I was also being rewarded for my courage not to sell out.

Jump for Joy to Preserve Your Spirit

My thoughts turned to those who are not able to protect their freedom as I had been able to do—people born into poverty, abuse, and climate-battered or war-torn countries. I thought as well of the captive dolphins who had lost their freedom the day of their captures. I realized that the second part of the "Jump for the joy of it" insight suggests that those who've already lost their freedom strive to jump for the joy of it anyway, in order to protect their spirits—the last bastion of their freedom.

A week later, I was incorporating some of my new publisher's editing suggestions and took my book bag filled with the manuscript to the beach to work on it in the sun. As I walked toward the small, but deep dolphin pool at the end of the lagoon near the restaurant, Kaiko'o rushed all the way to the edge of the pool and stood upright before me, then looked directly at me with a delighted look on his face. Next, he leaped his large body out of the small pool, keeping his eye on me as he jumped. Once his body was fully out of the water, he lifted his tail under himself with an exaggerated motion, as if to emphasize that he was jumping all the way out of the water. It seemed that Kaiko'o was using the sixth insight by jumping for the joy of it in order to protect the sovereignty of his spirit—even though he had lost his physical freedom long ago.

No longer concerned about what others might think, I hooted loudly and freely, as people gathered around the pool to see what was happening. Kaiko'o dashed over to the edge again and stood upright before me, looking very pleased with himself as his eyes twinkled happily into mine.

Then he went to the center of the pool to thrust himself fully out of the water again, but this time he flipped water at me with his tail, as he lifted it under him to clear the pool for another full jump. I laughed heartily as our eyes met again in recognition of what this meant. And again, he rushed over and stood upright before me, his face alight with pleasure and his chest flushed with pink.

To my amazement, Kaiko'o jumped once again, this time coming down with a big splash aimed in my direction, which soaked the rocks between us and caused his trainer to come over and ask Kaiko'o what was going on. He rushed over to me again and stood upright, as I squealed openly with delight and asked aloud if he could feel the joy. Kaiko'o executed two more full jumps, the last one reaching several feet into the air, before splashing more water on the rocks. He seemed to be truly enjoying himself, as I looked on with amazement and cheered with utter joy.

A sweet man with a heavy foreign accent approached me to ask, "What do you do to make the dolphin sing?"

I smiled as I clasped the book bag in my hand and paused before explaining, "He's remembering to jump for the joy of it."

Jump for the joy of it—with or without your freedom intact—then jump again, and again, and then again!

PART IV

A Change of Subject: Giving Back to the Dolphins and Whales

You cannot do a kindness too soon, for you never know how soon it will be too late.

—Unknown

Whenever we think of dolphins and whales, most of us invoke images of gleeful greetings, playful friendship, and frolicking fun, along with their gifts of humor, healing, rescue, and grace.

Many of you have had your own direct experience of this, while others have gleaned it vicariously while reading this book and others, or watching movies and video footage of cetacean magic. But, for whatever reason, most of the world seems to intuitively know that this tapestry of joy is simply who dolphins and whales are. Yet, in spite of their tireless ability to spin magic and stay loving under all kinds of circumstances, including our considerable abuses, the dolphins and whales now need our help!

I want to respond to this need by fulfilling a promise I made to them years ago. And, I want to do this now, by changing the subject in the next chapter to explain what the problem is and why the dolphins and whales need our help.

I first offered my promise to be of help to cetaceans after the Silver Bank whale made me aware that our military sonar is killing his family. But due to my personal conflict about going against our Navy—coupled with my own helplessness in the face of this potent technology manned by potent forces, I've simply not had the full measure of courage or strength needed to tackle this problem, nor have I had a means to deliver on my promise.

So, the purpose of this part of my book—before getting to the end of the cetacean's full story—is to make one last effort to follow the intense urgings of my heart to finally address this issue, and to do so by telling as much of the story as I know.

My goal is to clarify for as many people as possible that our military sonar technology is so intense that it's killing our marine life along with our ocean and ultimately ourselves if we continue to sit back and passively allow it.

To counter this possibility, I begin in the following chapter (16) to explain how I have come to terms with my own prior denial and resistance to telling this part of the cetacean narrative.

I then tell you the story of what was going on with the sonar during the period when the Silver Bank whale shared the news of its deadly impact on his family by giving me a personal taste of its power.

And, finally I provide an update on what happened next—and what is happening now—with the ongoing discharging of large amounts of sonar still going into our oceans, waterways, and inlets.

In chapter 17, I propose some ideas for how we have a real chance to reverse this problem if we band together to first face and then solve it with the formidable power of our Higher Selves.

We can become our Higher Selves most easily and effectively by enlisting the influence of a little known mechanism embedded in the base of each of our brains called "mirror neurons." These recently uncovered neurons—designed to impel us to mirror the behaviors that impress us the most—appear to have been designed to lure us toward becoming our best possibilities. They do this by enticing us to copy the most attractive qualities we have regular access to observing in charismatic leaders we feel close to and admire.

Yet, it appears that this design is being hijacked, due to so many people opting not to copy humanity's Higher Self traits and are more drawn to imitate our Lower Self options, which are taking us in increasingly dangerous directions.

To counter this highjacking, I offer several ways to lure our mirror neurons back to the side of our Higher Selves, hopefully in time to not just save ourselves, but to also experience the magic of being our best selves.

And, finally, the information I offer in chapter 18 offers us a preview of what we can collectively accomplish by redirecting our mirror neurons away from the unkind off-roads so many of us are now traveling back onto our

Higher Self roads. Not only do these loftier roads offer us new pathways to elevating our own kindness levels, but also offer us a chance to begin a Kindness Movement large enough to save ourselves and our world, simply by saturating it with love.

Kindness is contagious.

CHAPTER 16

What Is the Sonar Problem and What Can We Do About It?

It's never too late to be what we might have been.

—George Eliot

Toward the end of my decade of swimming with dolphins and whales in the wild, I learned that our Navy's sonar technology was killing these bright and beautiful beings in their ocean home—and now twenty years later, continues to kill them.

I became aware of this problem during my last swim with cetaceans outside of the country in the Silver Bank Whale Sanctuary off the Dominican Republic. But when upon returning home, my efforts to inspire my activist friends to help me intercede failed, I stepped back.

Yet, because I continued to feel haunted by my knowledge of this hidden holocaust and the metaphoric whistle

I had been handed, I felt driven to seek ways to either hand the whistle off to others or figure out how to blow it myself. The urgency of this internal drive ebbed and flowed over the years, but would kick in whenever a new mass global stranding was reported, usually in the back sections of our news.

In the midst of my struggle, I realized I had to come to terms with the conflict I felt—and still feel—about blowing the whistle myself, due to my close connections to Navy friends, both past and present.

My Special Connection to the Navy

I had grown up on a sugar plantation in Hawai'i next to the Barber's Point Naval Air Station, where I had spent most of my weekends as a guest at their wonderful and welcoming Officer's Beach Club and snack bar—with tennis facilities, a pool, and restaurant nearby. I enjoyed many years there surfing and playing volleyball or cards and games, while socializing with the officers and their families who welcomed me into their hearts and homes. They had not only offered me worldly conversation, fun, and kindness, they had also motivated me to live an even larger life than the one my own daring and bright parents could inspire. Their daughters were some of my best friends and their sons the focus of many teen crushes. My time in conversation, play, and laughter with these special friends I viewed as family was a source of great joy throughout my childhood, teen, and young adult years.

I continue to enjoy my many navy friends and take pride in having Navy Seals and pilots in my family and as friends. As a result of my close connection to so many naval people,

I know as well as anyone how kind and caring they can be and have thus felt confused by their place at the helm of the sonar program.

At first, I sought comfort in assuming they were unaware of the program's full impact and its danger to the ocean or perhaps that they earnestly believe their own assurances to the public of its benign nature.

I even wondered if the full extent of their sonar program fell under the auspices of a rogue operation driven by forces outside of their purview, possibly by the developer of its technology, who was obsessed with "his baby" from the time of its inception until his death early in 2019 at the age of 101. This enigmatic man received massive funding for his pet project and even had enough political capital to have been awarded a special Chair with the US Navy.

Regardless of who runs the program or who knows about it, or even who helps to pay for it, I finally had to face that at least some of the Navy's ranking members understand the truth about their sonar, though I still cling to my hope that most of them are either in the dark or in denial about the full extent of its power.

Whatever the status of their knowledge, it seems clear that using the sonar is a miscalculation in judgment and that re-blowing the whistle that has already been blown is comparable to an intervention with a cherished family member denying the power of a deadly substance or weapon and persisting in using it.

Why Blow the Whistle?

Mass dolphin and whale strandings (ranging in numbers from one to a thousand or more) have been occurring on a regular basis across the globe for the past two decades. And, even though these events rarely make the news, they are increasing dramatically in number and scope as the US Navy launches new and larger sonar programs. In addition to the horror of so much whale carnage dotting our beaches and ocean floors, their deaths—much like the deaths of the canaries in the coalmines—signal a serious and deadly problem in our world's oceans and in our souls.

The question is: Will we allow the sonar to continue on this course of killing the wonderful cetaceans and their ocean home—and ultimately ourselves in the mix? Or, will we rouse ourselves into consciousness and respond appropriately, and in time, to end this unkind and imminent threat to all planetary life?

My History with the Sonar

I first heard about our US Navy's sonar assault on the ocean and its marine life from a group of activists I had met while attending the Whales Alive Conference at the Four Seasons on Maui in April of 1998. The conference was just a short plane ride away from the Big Island's whale sanctuary, where the first Hawai'i-based sonar tests were paradoxically scheduled to take place in a few months.

Several of the activists at the conference were concerned about the selection of the whale nursery for testing the Navy's newly intense and louder version of their sonar technology nicknamed "the sound heard around the world," due to its ability to broadcast its sound thousands of miles from its many sources. Because of this new development in the sonar's strength, the activists were making plans to fly over to personally observe its impact on the cetaceans in their sanctuary. Since I hadn't seen much about these tests in the news, I had assumed their impact to have been negligible.

But, when a group of the activists gathered on Maui several months later at a second dolphin and whale meeting that I was attending, those who had observed the tests were abuzz about the distressing sights they had witnessed. Among other things, they saw dolphins huddling in groups to cry their way through it; whales having seizures; and naval divers being ordered out of the water due to seizures, followed by a new ruling that they are no longer allowed in the water when the sonar is on.

I was impressed with this collection of bright and caring activists made up of environmentalists, marine scientists, and attorneys who questioned the Navy's claim of the sonar's benign nature, and I felt honored by an invitation to join their anti-sonar cause and email list.

Ironically, just a few months after joining this group, I was concluding my decade of swimming throughout the world with dolphins and whales by heading to the Dominican Republic to swim in the Silver Bank Whale Sanctuary. As I describe in chapter 14, it was there that the humpback whale had brought the sonar problem to my attention when he blasted my lungs to the point of paralysis with his sonar before releasing them to gasp for air in the nick of time. With that gesture, the whale made it clear that the sonar is the thing that's killing his family and causing the rise in mass global strandings.

I couldn't wait to get home to share this information with my new activist friends, whom I assumed would be as disturbed by this information as I was. But instead, they resisted not only the source of my information, but the message itself and me in the mix. Although they were still strongly against the naval use of sonar, their focus remained fixed on the intensity of its metallic sounds screeching through the water and disturbing—or even deafening—the whales as it traveled. Yet, in spite of their awareness of the sonar's power, they rejected all possibility that it could also be lethal.

When some additional clues pointed to naval sonar being the source of cetacean deaths and deafness, I turned to the National Marine Fisheries Services (NMFS) and the National Oceanic and Atmospheric Administration (NOAA) for help. But both of these marine protection agencies also ignored me.

When I then went directly to the press, they also ignored me in favor of printing standard press releases supplied by the Navy and marine protection agencies, releases that all declared the strandings to be "mysteries our scientists are studying."

I began to smell a cover-up around the time I also realized I was unnervingly on my own, still holding that whistle that needed blowing. Yet, I had no idea how to blow it. And so, I rolled up my sleeves and did some serious research.

Hidden Reports and Hidden Problems

In the midst of my sleuthing, I ran across a chilling report, written fifty years earlier by the Marine Mammal Commission (an independent arm of the US government), requesting that all use of our naval sonar in the ocean be fully discontinued.

This was a disquieting discovery because the request had been issued on the heels of a mass stranding in Greece immediately following one of the US Navy's first ocean sonar tests as early as 1966. Yet, this swift and strong response to a sonar-induced stranding was not just ignored; the request had been mysteriously silenced and buried in an obscure report where it has remained on mute for the past fifty years.

Meanwhile, the sonar program has continued and expanded full speed ahead throughout the ocean as if the early mandate to halt it had never been made. Moreover, during this period of continued use, everyone seems to have forgotten that the sonar had been proven to be the force that had killed the Abaco whales.

Fortunately, the Marine Mammal Commision's buried report also revealed that if stranded whales' ears are saved and tested, the results are able to definitively prove whether or not the dead whales had been exposed to acoustic assault from the sonar. Yet, rather than perform these tests to help solve the mystery of what is killing so many whales, the NMFS staff has historically gone out of their way to avoid taking this step.

Over time, it became increasingly evident that the Navy and marine protection agencies were engaged in an improper alliance that resulted in the Navy being given illegal permits to harm—or kill—shockingly large numbers of whales. This went on for a span of thirteen years in the absence of the navy completing their first Environmental Impact Statement (EIS), required to assure environmental safety before permits can be legally issued.

Because the permits were thus illegally given, the use of the sonar during this period was also illegal. In response to this flagrant breaking of the rules, the top attorney for the Natural Resources Defense Council (NRDC—a strong environmentalist watchdog group) continually sued the Navy and the protection agencies. Because the NRDC was being supported by a number of eminent members such as the late John Kennedy, Jr.; his cousin Robert Kennedy; Pierce Brosnan; James Taylor; Jean-Michel Cousteau; Leonardo DiCaprio; and Robert Redford—they could afford to repeatedly sue the Navy.

As a result of these lawsuits, the NRDC was able to stall the full use of the sonar for many years and even came close to stopping it altogether with a suit that went all the way to the Supreme Court for secretly flooding waters off of California's coast with intense levels of sonar. They lost that suit in a conservative court, and the sonar continued and continues today. (See notes #6 and #7).

Beware the Beached Canaries: My Prediction

Although the activists dropped me from their inner circle email list soon after I told them about my extraordinary Silver Bank whale experience, I continued to receive their general newsletter. This enabled me to read their weekly marine reports, informing me of a shocking rise in global mass strandings that was not being reported in the news. Because of my experience with the Silver Bank whale, I suspected there might be a connection between these strandings and the sonar tests.

When I carefully researched each of these strandings, I discovered that most of them had followed on the heels of Navy sonar tests in the areas where the whales had died. So, I drafted a chart showing the geographic connections between these sonar tests and the nearby strandings to attach to an article I had written, titled, "Beware the Beached Canaries." Merging my tip from the whale with this research, I boldly proposed something nobody else had yet suggested: I proposed that the sonar appeared to be the thing killing so many whales. I then posted my article on the Internet in February of 2000 and also emailed it directly to the activists' general list. To my surprise several of the activists posted "Beware" on their websites, causing the article to go viral and giving me access to several media outlets.

But, the majority of the activists continued to be dismayed by what they steadfastly viewed as the "absurdity" of my claim that sound could kill whales and angrily disputed my theory, along with distancing themselves even further from me in order to protect their reputations as scientists.

I could actually understand where they were coming from and realized that I would soon be dropped from their general email list in addition to their private one. As a result, I was running out of time to convince this group of skilled scientists—able to perform the ear tests suggested by the Marine Mammal Commission—of the importance of doing this test to expose culpability. Yet, before I could convince them, I had to find a way to overcome their resistance to the idea that the force of sound traveling through water at high speeds could generate a wave powerful enough to inflict acoustic trauma to the whales' heads and ears.

Because I was convinced the ear tests would prove the Silver Bank whale to be right about the sonar being the cause of so many cetacean strandings, I was anxious to have the tests performed in order to either prove or disprove my theory.

So, I made one last effort to inspire these scientists to get the job done by sending their full email list a one-stanza ditty I knew they would find irritating, yet memorable. I selected the ditty platform, since one of their well-liked members was a ditty aficionado, who enjoyed entertaining the the activists with ones he had written. So, with nothing more to lose, I took the plunge and sent the following ditty:

"If you want no more tears,
then check their ears,
and you will have your answer."

I then suggested they, "Sing this ditty to any tune; but keep singing if you want to know what's killing the whales."

I knew my ditty would offer final "evidence" to the group that I was indeed the "crazy lady" they had assumed me to be. But I also knew that my suggestion for checking the whales' ears (embedded in my annoying jingle) would catch in their awareness and thus be remembered and hopefully acted on.

Planting this idea in the minds of the only group of environmental scientists able to perform the tests came too late for them to gather ear samples from the February of 2000 strandings. However, the idea was now seeded in their awareness, where it could sit until needed.

Coincidentally, the idea to preserve the ears for testing was utilized sooner than expected when a dramatic stranding erupted in March of 2000, only a month after my public prediction that the Navy's sonar had caused the February of 2000 stranding.

The preserved—and tested—ears from that second stranding in March of 2000 were able to prove that acoustic trauma from the sonar was indeed the culprit killing the whales. The Silver Bank whale had been right!

The Backstory

By early March of 2000, the NMFS had given the Navy enough illegal permits to allow them to harm—or kill—as many whales as needed to proceed with their plan to inject sonar into a sizable swath of the ocean. Thus, all was in place for this powerful technology—still untested for environmental safety—to be deployed in up to 70 to 80 percent of our world's oceans in accordance with the Navy's stated goal.

I felt uniquely alone in my awareness of the full power and horror of the sonar heading out to flood the ocean and kill whatever dolphins and whales (and other marine life) crossed its wide path—most of it falling dead on the sea floor, never to be witnessed or counted.

Then, on March 15, 2000, the Navy began its sonar exercises prematurely in the Great Bahama Canyon, which resulted in the entire pod of its resident beaked whales ending up on the basin floor of the Canyon, never to be seen again and presumed dead.

Eighteen of these acoustically assaulted and brain-injured whales and a few dolphins (many bleeding from their ears and eyes) managed to wend their way to the shore of the Abaco Islands in the Caribbean to strand and be counted before taking their last breaths.

The astonishing coincidence was that some of these Bahamian cetaceans, outside the jurisdiction of the NMFS, selected the beachfront property of possibly the only maverick marine scientist uniquely qualified to prepare their ears for testing. He was someone these whales knew, since he had been studying them for the past decade—which suggests their selection may have been conscious, in accordance with their level of awareness and intelligence.

In fact, some speculate that all stranded whales die on our beaches to make a statement, rather than fall to the ocean's floor to die without human knowledge. If this is true, it leaves us to wonder how many dead cetaceans never make it to shore and are, instead, forming ocean floor graveyards, as some divers have seen, following Navy sonar exercises. One of these graveyards was memorialized during a naval public hearing held in Hawai'i when a female diver tearfully shared the mass of bones she and her companion saw off Catalina Island following sonar exercises nearby.

Thus, the only remaining barrier to getting these whales' ears tested was that the maverick scientist was a fiercely loyal Navy man who was conflicted between his love for the whales and his love for the Navy. He was also one of the activists who had found me particularly annoying and was unaware that I was also conflicted, due to my own close connections to Navy people.

Yet, the maverick was acutely aware (possibly in part due to my annoying ditty) that getting fresh ear samples was essential to solving the mystery of why so many whales were dying, and if their deaths were in fact due to the sonar.

As fate would have it, when the maverick's whale friends began to land on his beachfront property to die at his feet, his heart was moved to help them. So, rather than risk *not* having their ears checked by calling the NMFS, he decided to keep these whales under Bahamian jurisdiction and use his own skills to remove their heads and prepare their ears for testing.

With this decision, the maverick scientist became the hero who set in motion the attainment of solid evidence that would reveal the undeniable connection between cetacean sonar exposure and the surge of cetacean strandings and deaths.

He and his camera also had a front row seat to the truth of what these tests revealed, so when the Navy's ear specialist inadvertently exposed her plan to obscure the results, the maverick risked both his career and his ties to the Navy to preempt her results and blow the whistle himself.

He did this by showing his videos to the press of the bloody impact the explosive concussions had rendered on the ears and brains of these whales he knew had been exposed to a naval sonar exercise. He knew this because he had seen a naval ship (carrying its sonar equipment) leaving the area earlier that day. It was a shattering sight that forced him to face that his beloved Navy was, in fact, killing the whales.

The maverick's brave whistleblowing culminated in an interview on *60 Minutes* that alerted the public to the truth about the US Navy's sonar causing cetacean strandings. The clarity of his proof could never be recalled or hidden again. It was a bell that simply could not be unrung!

Then, to ring the bell even louder, Living Planet Books publisher, Joshua Horwitz, wrote a bestselling page-turner— *War of the Whales, A True Story*—in which he masterfully weaves the scientist's story as told in his own words into the NRDC attorney's stories about his lawsuits against the US Navy's persistently illegal use of the sonar. (See Notes #6 and #7)

Yet, in spite of these facts shared on 60 minutes and again in Horwitz's book, the maverick's proof seems to have been forgotten and the bell "unrung," since his discovery is almost never mentioned when whales strand. Nor is a connection between strandings and the sonar included in the current press releases submitted by the Navy, NMFS, and NOAA.

Instead, their reports inform us that animal autopsies (called necropsies) will be performed to see what might be killing so many whales, even though they know that necropsies are far less able than ear tests using CT scans to uncover whether or not sonar is the offender that's acoustically assaulting the whales.

Moreover, the "experts" tend only to mention the deep diving beaked whales when discussing whale deaths connected to the sonar and blame it on their rapid surfacing from their deep-water habitats and thus getting the bends. They fail to mention that the Abaco Island beaked whales were proven to have died from acoustic assault to their heads—rather than the bends—and that sonar, not the bends, is the real issue. Nor do they discuss the many other species of dolphins and whales killed from sonar exposure or that acoustic assault can also deafen the whales, resulting in deadly collisions with boats.

Neither do their reports mention the grave problem of the sonar killing keystone marine plants such as algae—essential to the life of coral—or kelp needed as a food source for a wide array of marine life. Because of these serious omissions, people are not aware that sonar is in the water or of the impact it's having on all marine life and the domino effect this can have on the algae, kelp, and coral keystones of our ocean's and world's ecosystems as explained in *The Serengeti Rules* by Sean B. Carroll.

So, how did we get from clear disclosure about the Abaco purging of the Grand Canyon whales to a return to denial? Perhaps a brief summary of the events that followed the Abaco exposé will help to reveal how the truth about the deadly impact of the sonar on our marine life and ocean went dark again.

Events Following the Unmasking of the Sonar

The proof of the whales' mass execution by sonar in the Bahamas in March of 2000 prompted Congress to pass a bill in 2001 banning all further use of Navy sonar. But, a few months later, 9/11 hit, and America went to war. Then due to our being at war, Congress exempted the US military from adhering to all marine laws protecting the ocean, which enabled the sonar to return to the water with even greater force and less restraint.

Now, two decades later as *Compelling Conversations* goes to press, the Navy's sonar program not only continues, but is robustly expanding with new additions such as the Navy's Northwest Training and Testing program—a program that discharges additional sonar into the west coast waterways and Pacific Ocean.

Since the launch of this program in 2015, disposing of whale carcasses has become a new and growing challenge, with more dead whales on the way. Tragically, this new phenomenon of serial cetacean death is on course to continue for as long as we're engaged in a war somewhere in the world, since the United States being at war enables our navy to "legitimately" ignore all marine laws. So, unless we change our view that peppering our ocean with lethal military weaponry and using it for war practice is what keeps us safe, we risk losing all of our cetaceans and other marine life, and ultimately the ocean and much more.

The situation reminds me of the dolphins' sixth insight: Arrange for your freedom before it's too late! And, that's what this section of the book is about. It's time to arrange for our freedom along with arranging for our survival!

Additional Consequences of Navy Sonar

In addition to the assault Navy sonar wages on our marine life that we know about, there are other equally serious problems the sonar also appears to be causing.

For example, there have been increasing reports of a number of disturbing sonar-related events, including such things as: a decline in the ocean's algae required for coral health; subsequent coral bleaching; and the death of coral beds in areas where the sonar is most active. Because sonar is known to kill algae—and is even used for intentionally killing algae overgrowth in ponds—a strong case can be made that the use of sonar in our oceans is causing the death of ocean algae and the subsequent death of coral beds, essential to the life of the ocean. (See Note #7.)

Even More and Potentially Bigger Problems

In addition to the problems we know about, such as cetacean death, and those we suspect, such as coral death, there's a good chance sonar is also causing a number of other less visible, but potentially even more catastrophic problems. This is due to the reality that sonar heats the ocean as it travels rapidly through the water up to a thousand miles from its many sources (ironically, to measure ocean temperatures, among other things). (See Note #8.)

When we pair this unknown amount of ocean heating with the Navy's goal of injecting sonar into 70 to 80 percent of the world's oceans, it's clear that sonar is contributing to the rise in ocean temperatures, though we don't know by how much. If this is correct—and depending on the degree of heat it generates—the sonar is also contributing to climate change and all the disruption and chaos that entails.

Finally Blowing the Whistle with Renewed Intent and Fresh Hope

As a result of my acute interest in the sonar following my day with the Silver Bank whale, I immersed myself in the available research and learned a good deal about the who, where, and why of our national sonar assault on the ocean, in spite of its destructive effect on our planet. And the more I learned, the harder it became to simply hold onto the whistle I had been handed without forming some kind of a plan. So, I faced my need to either pass off the whistle to someone else to blow or to blow it myself before any more damage is done. Gratefully, once I made this commitment, several ideas for how to blow it came to me.

That's when I decided to more vividly reveal the dolphins' insights on how humanity can draw increased levels of goodness and grace to our hearts to then send to our world during this pinnacle period in all of our lives. So, I revised and revitalized this final edition of my book chronicling my enchanting experiences with the cetaceans, but this time with added information and new intent.

I decided to also more fully include the story of the ceaseless bloodbath beneath the sea that the dolphins and whales are forced to endure in hopes of inspiring others to correct this injustice that serves as a hologram of the many injustices we inflict on others.

Next, I explain how our Higher Selves can develop more rapidly than we've been led to believe and then virally spread to others by more consciously employing the power of our "mirror neurons," as described in the following chapter (17). The conscious partnership I propose we develop with these newly discovered and unusual neurons offers us a new path to humanity's improvement and a fresh chance for *real* hope.

I further vowed never to let up on being my own best self or doing what I can to inspire my species to become a more loving humanity. My passion to do better was spawned during my time with the dolphins and whales, who constantly clarified that the power of love is the most crucial element for living in joy and healing our world. It's also the *only* path to saving ourselves, as futurist Bucky Fuller declared in his last public talk.

Bucky—as he liked to be called—exposed this truth as he often did, following several moments on stage with his eyes closed and hands clasped to his chest as he tuned his heart into the wisdom of the Universe. He would then open his eyes to share what he had just received, and on this occasion, the healthy octogenarian also shared that he would die in a few days in order to accompany his dying wife of sixty years, which he did.

Bucky ended this last of his talks in 1983 by pleading with us to take heed regarding the reality that we simply won't make it unless we become loving, the same verdict decreed by all great spiritual and secular leaders. It's also the scientific conclusion drawn by the Stanford University-based Heartmath Institute, a science organization founded in 1991, eight years after Bucky's death and soon after the dolphins began their first tutorials with me on the power of being loving.

Because humanity failed to heed this warning from multiple sources when offered three decades ago, we are now seeing a preview of what can and will happen if we don't figure out how to be loving. Yet, in spite of our failure to act on this forewarning, the dolphins and whales haven't given up on us and continue to vigorously share their message that love is everything and that without it we have nothing. It's no wonder that both the dolphins and whales continue to dance their hearts out for us at every opportunity in an effort to beguile us into joining them in simply being loving.

As Bucky Fuller begged his final audience not to give up on trying to be our best selves, his last words were, "So, darling people, please don't let up!"

—Bucky Fuller

CHAPTER 17

Real Hope For Humanity

*With tender patience, the dolphins hug our
shores to dance for us, play with us, and
win us over to love.*

I
t was toward the end of my decade filled with loving
and kind exchanges with the dolphins and whales that I
was alarmed to learn about my species waging a sonar
assault on them and their ocean home. As a result of the
timing and unusual way I learned of our unkindness to these
gentle souls living beneath the sea, I wondered why humans
would make such a choice. I also wondered why, in contrast
to the consistently Higher Self behaviors of the cetaceans,
so many of us seemed callously drawn to being our Lower
Selves.

As I further noticed where these unkind roads were leading and where they have brought us to date, I concluded that
a big enough split between our Lower and Higher Selves

has developed to cloud which of these Selves represents who we are. It's also unclear which Self we will nurture as we collectively stand at this vital fork in the road of our destiny and if we have the will to pursue our Higher Selves. In fact, there seems to be a war between these two possibilities for the future of humanity, and it's unnervingly unclear which side will win.

The Course of Our Unkindness

As I studied how and why so many unkind groups were forming in my human society and why they were able to entice so many followers, I noticed that these unkind groups all have one disturbing quality in common. They seem to begin with strongly narcissistic individuals or small groups of greedy and self-centered people who've managed to overtake and dominate the stages and spotlights of our homes, our schools, and much of our adult society. The goal they all seem to share in common is a need to diminish, hurt, and dominate others in order to elevate their own status and primacy and to be viewed as having great power and importance.

Yet, their "importance" doesn't come from any real greatness or talent, but from their smallness and meanness. Moreover, because the origin of their "importance" lies in treating others badly, it's comparable to the "faux" power of the bullies and mean girls in our schools and the self-appointed "superior" men and women in our adult society.

When others naively fall for their claims and copy their meanness in hopes of sharing in their faux status, it adds to the illusion for them—and for others observing them—that they really are part of an elite group and in possession of the privilege and power they falsely claim.

As a result, even some of the nice kids at school and the kind adults in our society are drawn to the scam and alter their behavior in order to be part of this growing fad of unkindness and share in the forged power and popularity that goes with it. Unfortunately, these new followers serve to attract even more followers and so on, as the group expands into dangerously large numbers. Others may not copy their meanness, but remain silent in its presence due to their fear that it will be turned on them. The tragedy of this option is that those who remain mute fail to realize how many of the people observing their silence will be inclined to copy it. In short, those who choose silence inadvertently give permission to other good people to remain passively quiet while a rise in evil flourishes around them.

So, why does this happen? Why on earth would so many of us follow—or remain complicitly silent—in the presence of the mean kids at school and the vicious adults in our society, since doing so supports a precarious trend of behaving as our Lower Selves? And, why have these trends flourished in our past during periods when suppression and cruelty of others have prevailed? And why is it still happening in so many forms today, such as our unkindness toward each other, toward other species, and even toward our own planetary home?

So, I ask again, why on earth would anyone copy the bullies and boors in our midst, or remain silent while observing their cruel acts, rather than stop them before they have a chance to get their footing and stake a claim in our hearts, our homes, and our world as we travel together on this shared planet and journey of life? Why on earth would any of us want to be part of a trend leading to our own self-degradation and destruction? The answer to this long and generational mystery lies in the unseen power of our "mirror neurons," quietly hiding at the base of each of our brains.

How Mirror Neurons Work

The incongruity of the mean kids in our schools and the cruel adults in our society attracting so many followers and becoming a popular trend made no sense to me. That is, it made no sense until I learned about our "mirror neurons" or "sponge neurons," as Neuropsychiatrist, Dr. Dan Siegel, so aptly calls them. The reason Dr. Siegel nicknamed mirror neurons "sponge" neurons is because of their surprising role in influencing us to mimic or "soak up" the attitudes and behaviors of the people we're observing, even when those attitudes and actions are unkind and don't match our own moral compass.

What is the mechanism that enables sponge neurons to prompt us to copy the things we see and thus influence our own behavior and the character of our culture—whether for good or for bad? How is it that who we are as individuals or a society depends on who or what has caught the attention of our mirror neurons and then dazzled them into wanting to support or copy what they were reflectively seeing? Here's how it works.

Because our mirror neurons fire in the exact same cerebral location and sequence in our brains that are firing in the brains of the people we're observing, we're able to "mirror" or reflectively sense what those people are feeling and to thus feel an affinity to them. Whenever the people we feel this initial connection to are also able to impress us and win our trust, we experience an unexpected urge to copy their attitudes and behaviors and to generally be like them. Interestingly, this can happen when observing an athlete scholar or the class clown…or when in the presence of a genuinely kind mentor or a charming sociopath.

Accordingly, on those occasions when our mirror neurons beguile us to copy worthy role models who lead us to our best selves, they are working as designed; but during those times when they go astray, our mirror neurons tempt us to follow dangerously cruel, yet charismatic influencers down perilously dark roads.

When Mirror Neurons are Working as Designed

Whenever children feel close enough to their own kind families to trust and use their guidance, their mirror neurons are working as they are meant to work and for the benefit of all: the children, their families, and our society.

To do all we can to secure this result, in addition to families being consistently kind, it's essential that they also know how to gently employ fair rules, since it's this combination that triggers their children's desire to be like them. It's also this blend that stimulates high levels of confidence, cooperation, and brightness in children—a mixture that equips them to discern the lack of real power in the bullies at school and to find them unappealing and annoying, rather than someone to copy.

Accordingly, the best way to discourage children's mirror neurons from the pull to copy the bullies and boors of our society is to nurture their feelings of closeness to kind families and adults who are also clear about fair rules. Not surprisingly, the opposite is also true.

In spite of how well nature has designed this pathway to a High Level humanity, many parents and others in our society encumber the design by failing to offer children a balance of reliable boundaries steeped in the gentleness of love. Instead, they may strive to parent primarily from either the nurturing or discipline side, but end up swinging between the two extremes in an effort to gain control over children when they challenge fair rules, sometimes coddling them and sometimes yelling or even hitting (as reported by 65% of parents).

Such pendulum parenting usually results in a child's mirror neurons failing to trigger feelings of secure attachment and closeness to his or her family or a desire to be anything like them. Instead, such children become vulnerable to copying the mean kids at school who may offer more consistency and appeal for them than their unpredictable families.

Learning from the Cetaceans

In contrast to our societal confusion about the value of offering both parental love and firm boundaries, cetaceans are not only clear about the importance of their rules, but are equally clear about how to calmly, yet firmly, hold them.

You may recall from Chapter 5 that a woman invading a resting whale's space was given the same consequence the whale's own child would have received—that of being held under water until parental dominance and the authority to lead was made clear. It was a consequence unpleasant enough to assure the cetacean child's surrender to his rules.

But, it was also applied with a gentle and anger-free energy of calm that would enable him to understand that love had not been abandoned; the rules were simply also being held. Interestingly, it's this calm balance between love and enforced rules that results in cetacean children respecting parental authority, while also wanting to be like their families and an integral part of their familial group.

Although holding uncooperative children under water works for whales, humans will need to find alternative methods and can consult *Parachutes for Parents* for guidance in how to simultaneously and consistently maintain both love and boundaries.

Once we create these kinds of conditions that invite our mirror neurons to work as designed in our homes and schools as well as in our adult society, the majority of us will feel a steady pull to follow our family and societal leaders traveling cooperatively in the lanes of their Higher Selves.

But, until that time comes, we need to each decide if we want to become a Higher or Lower Self person and to then guide our mirror neurons to seek out and follow only those who have made the same choice. If we fail to actively involve ourselves in vigilantly making this choice at this uncertain time in our history, we will be left by omission with a collection of unkind and dominant people leading us to our Lower Selves and ultimate self-destruction.

Will We Choose to be a Higher or Lower Self Society

Clearly, the potent pull for both children and adults to imitate the behaviors of the most visible people in the spotlights and on the stages of our society causes those we are copying to become even more admired with a growing following and more visibility and power. As a result, both individuals and groups can become either an inspiring beam for good or a powerful force for evil, pulling large segments of society in the direction of either their Higher or Lower Selves.

This helps to explain why we've taken a number of historical paths leading to periods of intellectual excellence, heart-driven kindness, and cultural renaissance juxtaposed to some horrifically cruel and callous roads in our human history—including female and minority suppression, child abuse, genocide, slavery, the Holocaust, and now a new and growing tolerance for the degradation and even the annihilation of each other, other species, our ocean, our planet, and ourselves. These dark paths take hold during times when they are passively tolerated and then copied by growing numbers of followers—rather than stopped in their early stages.

If we are content to be a Lower Self society, then continuing to passively allow cruelty or even actively copying it will surely lead us down that road. Yet, once there, we will be forced to deal with the intractable problems that cruelty engenders, including such things as social, gender, and racial injustice; chaos and violence; rampant disease, ocean death, planetary collapse, and ultimately, our own annihilation.

But, if we care about being a heart-driven, Higher Self society—able to guide our futures toward kindness, safety, and grace—then making sure our mirror neurons are being triggered only by genuinely Higher Self leaders is critical to our lives and futures. Let me repeat: Making sure our mirror neurons are being triggered only by genuinely Higher

Self leaders is critical to our lives and futures…and to our survival.

So, as we stand at a crucial crossroad in the history of humanity as we know it, what can we do to step back from the cliff we seem to have reached as a result of passively allowing or, at times, even actively following the Lower Self bullies and cruel leaders in our midst?

Choosing to Be a Higher Self Society

In lieu of blindly following the Lower Self bullies and malicious leaders among us in lemming-like fashion, what else might we do in the event we decide we want to be a Higher Self society? What can we do to make that happen? How can we make sure we're copying the genuinely kind and noble leaders following the path to our Higher Selves?

Actively Getting the "Faux" Leaders off the Stage

The best way to assure that we're using our mirror neurons to their greatest advantage is to kindly—and I repeat kindly—remove the bullies and boors from the stages and spotlights in our homes and schools, as well as in our adult society. This not only prevents the "faux leaders" from triggering our children's or our own mirror neurons to imitate humanity's lower self qualities, it also makes room for true Higher Self leaders to take the stage and lead us to higher ground. So, how can we do this, and what would it look like?

We can best accomplish the purging of the rule-breakers' and bullies' antics from the view of our children's and our own mirror neurons by more immediately—yet legally, kindly, and gently—removing them for a time-out from the living rooms, classrooms, and playgrounds of our homes and schools as well as from our adult society. We must then guard against prematurely returning these people to the group before they have genuinely surrendered to conforming to our societal standards of kindness and cooperation at a level we can trust.

In addition to eliminating the visibility of the uncooperative and unkind behaviors that stimulate the mirror neurons of our children and ourselves, it's essential to replace these disruptive activities with truly inspiring Higher Self leaders able to guide us toward our best selves. Thus, in conjunction with getting the rule-breakers and bullies out of our view, we can more actively arrange to expose our mirror neurons to people imbued with the same type of just wisdom, kindness, grace, and joy that we observe in the cetacean souls living harmoniously beneath the surface of the water not far from our shores.

Creating More Higher Self Leaders to Copy

There are many individuals, groups, and movements already underway that are striving to inspire these qualities of the Higher Self within each of us individually and in the best interests of our society. Yet, these groups are often not visible or large enough to draw the attention needed to trigger the mirror neurons of enough others to make a real difference. To remedy this weakness, some of these groups might want to align with others to become a genuinely stronger, more visible and dynamic force—or a superpod—traveling with others on the same path in the lanes of the Higher Self.

A Kindness Movement

If enough of us join these lanes of the Higher Self, we can create a super highway large enough to form a Kindness Movement generating exponentially more and more of the magnetic energy of love, similar to what the dolphins and whales do when they travel and play together in large superpod groups consisting of a collection of their various smaller groups.

If enough of us add our energies and ideas to those of other people going in the same direction, we have a chance to generate a powerful movement of kindness moving through our hearts and into the world as a larger body—or a substantial Movement of human kindness.

My personal contribution to increasing the traffic flow of the Higher Self begins first with my own development and then with this book (and my other books). I also intend to expose the sonar story in a film, cast with notably charismatic and popular celebrities able to engage the Higher Self mirror neurons of millions of people in their audiences.

Once started, all of our combined contributions to becoming our best selves and a greater humanity—whether quiet and personal or more publicly displayed—will come together to forge new lanes filled with people sharing the qualities of the Higher Self. These lanes will not only grow, but will ultimately converge to bring humanity into alignment with our soul-selves as we travel together toward living in our greatness and healing our world.

We can make this happen by collectively adopting the Higher Self traits that the dolphins model for us, coupled with using their manifesting insights to realize the lives we most want to live in the world we most want to inhabit.

The only remaining question is this: Will we do it in time to enjoy the ultimate experience of our own Higher Selves as well as endure as a species by saving the cetaceans, the ocean, the planet, and ourselves? Will we form a loving and just coalition with the size, savvy, and determination to insure that the will of the heart overcomes the illusive power of those who gain from continued chaos and cultural suicide?

As we organize ourselves around this goal, the dolphins and whales offer us a touchstone of love as seen in the following chapter.

With tender patience, the dolphins hug our
shores to dance for us, play with us and win
us over to our greatness.

CHAPTER 18

Our Greatest Teachers Live Their Message of Love

Cetaceans offer the world a touchstone of love.

During the period when the sonar was flooding the ocean on a more regular basis and the Hawai'i cetaceans were especially challenged by its assaults, a group of orcas in the San Juan Islands were regularly showing up in time for concerts planned for their benefit by the whale-loving musician, Jim Nollman, and his band.

These orcas not only appreciated the human musicians playing for them, but actively and playfully joined in the singing.

Farther down the coast, a superpod of whales numbering in the thousands showed up off the shores of Dana Point in Southern California. They interacted with people in their leisure boats, staying with them until sunset, at which time the entire pod lay still on the surface as the sun set on a sea filled with dorsal fins seeming to bid a dramatic adieu to their new human friends.

And across the ocean, South African dolphins joined an international surfing contest—playfully outperforming the human surfers—that was viewed with amusement and amazement on various devices by people throughout the world.

The dolphins and whales remain primarily kind and gentle with us, forever willing to play and help and teach us, no matter what we do to them. Like others who have reached similarly high states of evolution, they seem to be waiting patiently for our hearts to open and our interconnectedness and consciousness to awaken. They also seem to know that their presence in our lives will accelerate our ability to become more aware, conscious, and kind, and so they continue to come to our boats and shores, seeking us out and helping us to heal and evolve toward our highest potential.

Cetaceans as Consistently Higher Self Beings

Although their survival—along with ours—depends on our hearts being moved enough to act in resonance with our Higher Selves, cetaceans are also clear that they will remain who they are, whether or not we succeed in becoming kinder to each other and to them.

Dolphins can swim, jump, and spin higher and faster than is comprehensible for their size and configuration. Whales pull forty to fifty tons out of the water's depth to present themselves with amazing grace. Both arrive out of nowhere in answer to a thought, a prearranged encounter, or a need for healing or rescue.

They're filled with kind compassion, harmony, and joyful grace, and they speak through multiple channels at ultrasonic wavelengths. When we can't understand, they find a way to get through. They heal, they bring joy, and they evoke awe and bliss. They are quite simply among the greatest beings in our midst.

Throughout this book, I've shared stories of how the dolphins have modeled the traits of the Higher Self for us to see and copy, in addition to designing a prescription for how we, too, can manifest our own world of beauty and greatness.

By focusing only on being their best, dolphins and whales create a powerful force field of clarity and joy and then bring that field to our shores to share with us, while using it to heal, teach, and pull us into it. Their generous interactions with us not only stir and open our hearts, but stretch us to become more as they wait patiently for us to join them at the level they've attained.

In their presence, we think of Spirit, or God, and feel pulled into the vibration of our highest potential. When we accept these great beings as teachers and not only learn from them, but also copy their example of how to embody our own ability to love all things at all times, the energy we generate from this invisible power will prove to be a force so strong it can twirl whales and spin galaxies.

If we're willing to let go of our lesser selves, who have become such familiar and long-term companions, in order to embrace and mirror the lessons the dolphins come to our shores to model and teach, we will not only uncover the power of love, we will also fulfill our purpose by pulling the joy of heaven through our hearts to our earth home and lives.

Dolphins and whales sing beneath the sea and dance across the horizon, beguiling us to join them in their ballet of wisdom, love, harmony, and joy—waiting patiently for us to arrive.

Notes

1. Emotional Freedom Technique (EFT) is a trauma treatment technique (developed and generously shared with the world by Gary Craig) that employs the use of tapping on specific points on the body.

2. Ken Marten, Karim Shariff, Suchi Psarakos, and Don J. White, "Ring Bubbles of Dolphins," *Scientific American* 275, no. 2 (August 1996): 82–87.

3. Information on the double, triple, and quadruple helices can be found in Jonathan Amos, "Quadruple Helix DNA Seen in Human Cells," BBC News, Science and Environment, January 20, 2013.

4. Sonoluminescence is a discovery made by physicists who found that bubbles bombarded with high-frequency sonar emit blue light. This bombardment is believed to be able to conduct a very intense degree of heat, possibly even a source of cold fusion. I periodically saw beautiful blue lighted bubbles in the water on days when the dolphins were near, and one of these appeared to be the cause of a small patch of water about a foot in front of me to bubble on the ocean's surface for about thirty seconds, while also emitting a white vapor, similar to the vapor seen in dry ice.

5. James Nestor, author of Deep: *Freediving, Renegade Science, and What the Ocean tells Us about Ourselves*, reports that the free divers he studied experienced sperm whales vibrating them to the point of temporarily paralyzing one man's arm and others feeling as though they could be vibrated to death. The vibrating also periodically raised the body temperatures of the divers. Further study of this information may help to explain the vibration I also experienced within my body soon after being sent extra energy from some large dolphins in Hawaiian waters, which resulted in my having a life-changing experience of newly deep feelings of caring for others.

6. Joel Reynolds, serving as an attorney for the National Resources Defense Council (NRDC), is the attorney who stalled the sonar assault on our ocean for many years with his multiple environmental lawsuits against them. Robert Redford, Leonardo DiCaprio, and James Taylor are current members of the NRDC"s Board of Trustees and Tom Steyer is an active supporter of this persistent protector of our environment. (www.nrdc.org)

7. Details of this and other fascinating and mystery-laden stories about the sonar, told from the perspectives of the maverick scientist and NRDC attorney, can be found in Joshua Horwitz' wonderful, page-turning *War of the Whales: A True Story*.

8. During submarine sonar experiments, it was noticed that the complex pattern of ultrasonic vibrations through the water causes the vacuole cell wall of algae to resonate and break, much in the way high-pitched sounds can cause a

glass to break. The broken vacuole wall eliminates its ability to grow and reproduce, which presumably threatens all marine plants, since they all have vacuoles.

9. The reason sound can travel so much faster and farther through water than through air is that it's converted to heat—primarily by the Epsom salt dissolved in seawater—though the exact amount of ocean heating generated from the sonar is unnervingly unknown to us.

10. For more information on my ebook, *Manifest!,* describing my dolphin-inspired manifesting program in greater detail, go directly to Amazon.com or MakingRelationshipsWork.com

Resources for Swimming with Dolphins and Whales

Anne Gordon. Anne Gordon is a highly experienced and successful cetacean retreat leader. She leads Whale and Dolphin Wisdom Retreats around the world in places like the Pearl Islands, Panama; Baja, Mexico; Bimini, Bahamas; Mo'orea, French Polynesia; the San Juan Islands, and Kealakekua, Hawaii. Anne loves nothing more than to help you connect, commune, and learn from the dolphins and whales as well as swim and play with them in the water and from boats. Anne was previously an animal trainer for the film industry and describes herself as a dolphin expert and a whale wisdom specialist.
Website: www.WhaleandDolphinWisdomRetreats.com
Email: Anne@WhaleWatchingPanama.com

Tori Cullins. Tori Cullins is the best tour guide on O'ahu. Tori and her husband, Armin Cullins, are delightful, heart-centered people and the owners of Wild Side Specialty Tours. They are also concerned about the mounting problems in the ocean and do all they can to raise awareness and be of help. A portion of their proceeds goes to the non-profit Wild Dolphin Foundation.
Website: http://sailhawaii.com
Email: WildSide@SailHawaii.com Tel: 808-306-7273

WildQuest, The Human Dolphin Connection. I did not swim with WildQuest, The Human Dolphin Connection, a Bimini resource, but they graciously connected me to another boat when theirs was damaged in a storm. Owned by Amlas McLeod and Atmo Kubesa, WildQuest provides dolphin tours that periodically include specialists to provide a spiritually based platform in areas such as meditation and yoga.

Website: www.wildquest.com/contact

Email: reservations@wildquest.com / Tel: 800-326-1618

Jan Salerno. Jan Salerno of Dolphin Whisperers Hawai'i is located in Kona, Hawai'i. The recipient of consistently strong, favorable reviews, Jan hosts small and large groups to connect with Big Island dolphins and whales in accordance with the established Marine Sanctuary guidelines. She is also an IDC Staff Scuba Instructor with PADI and is on the board of directors of WHALE RN (West Hawaii Aquatic Large Entanglement Response Network). Jan previously worked in diving throughout the Caribbean, South Pacific, Hawaii, and Southern California and is clearly passionate about all marine life and their ocean home.

Website: www.dolphinwhisperershawaii.com

Email: Jan@DolphinWhisperersHawaii.com /

Tel. 619-309-5236

About The Author

Bobbie Merrill is a child and family therapist, parenting consultant, and trauma treatment specialist. She is also a bestselling international author as well as a past contributor to an award-winning Relationship Column for the *Honolulu Advertiser* and a freelance Relationship columnist with her husband, Dr. Tom Merrill, for Cox News/NY Times News Service.

Bobbie was honored in *Honolulu Magazine* at the height of her career as one of Honolulu's most successful women. Now a grandmother and a conscious female voice, Bobbie continues to remain passionate about inspiring all of us—herself included—to become our best selves in order to create a kinder, more just and joyful humanity living in a kinder, more just and joyful world. To this end, Bobbie continues to write books and blogs, consult, and conduct online classes designed to help us bring these possibilities to life.

Bobbie feels blessed to have been born in paradise into an adventurous and fun-loving family living on the beautiful Waianae Coast of Oʻahu when Hawaiʻi was still a United States Territory. Later growing up on a sugar plantation adjacent to her birthplace, she commuted to Honolulu to attend private school, which she credits for broadening her societal and academic horizons. Her weekends were filled with competitive swim meets as well as surfing and playing tennis and beach volleyball with friends.

At the age of fifteen, Bobbie's first summer job at the pineapple cannery (before later working as a swim instructor) gratefully awakened her to the reality of social and racial injustice, a lesson that that has strongly informed her heart and influenced her life and work.

Following two years of college on the West Coast, Bobbie spent her junior year studying literature and art at the Institute for American Universities in Aix-en-Provence, France, where she also enjoyed further awakening and extensive travel throughout Europe. She returned to the United States to graduate with a major in English literature from Wayne State University, followed by earning a graduate degree in education at San Jose State College and then teaching English literature at a Palo Alto high school.

Bobbie eventually returned to her Hawaii roots to raise her children and resume playing competitive tennis and social golf with friends, while earning a master's degree in clinical social work at the University of Hawaii, which included completing advanced training in child development, trauma treatment, and conflict resolution.

Trained as a child and adult therapist and parenting coach, Bobbie focused her career on early childhood development, coupled with private adult counseling. She also co-founded the socio-emotional development program at the Unity School of Hawai'i, a prominent, progressive preschool known for its notably loving students consistently scoring in the superior range on entrance examinations to Honolulu's rigorous private schools.

Bobbie's best-selling book, *Parachutes for Parents,* describing her method, is widely used by parents and teachers and as a text at a number of colleges. Bobbie has taught her program to parents and staff at numerous private and public schools throughout the United States and currently conducts online parenting classes with her husband. They also hold partnership success classes based on their book, *Settle for More, You <u>Can</u> Have the Relationship you Always Wanted ... Guaranteed!*

Once her children were off to college, Bobbie returned to the waters of her birthplace to celebrate her fiftieth birthday by swimming with the Waianae spinners, making her among the first to swim with dolphins in the wild. She went on to enjoy a decade-long journey of over two thousand hours of free swimming with dolphins and whales in unique travel destinations throughout the world. Her book, *Compelling Conversations with Dolphins and Whales in the Wild: Vital Lessons for Living in Joy and Healing Our World* offers readers a rare opportunity to vicariously experience her entrancing adventure and its potent lessons.

Bobbie has two adult children and three grandsons—all of whom she describes as being uniquely "kind, bright, talented, and fun people." Bobbie is a world traveler who currently lives and works in close partnership with her husband and soul partner near Seattle and Puget Sound, where the orcas live.

You can contact Bobbie to sign up for her parenting and/or partnership classes at www.MakingRelationshipsWork.com.

Made in the USA
Las Vegas, NV
07 November 2022

58965672R00173